WAR AND PEACE IN POST-COLONIAL CEYLON
1948-1991

War and Peace in Post-Colonial Ceylon
1948-1991

Errata

Adrian Wijemanne : War and Peace in Post-Colonial
Ceylon 1948-1991

Page 18, last line
After "Just prior to" — read "Independence, and the one with the best
democratic credentials of ".

Page 80, last line
After "bound-" read "ed; boundaries and minorities".

Orient Longman

WAR AND PEACE IN POST-COLONIAL CEYLON: 1948-1991

Orient Longman Limited

Registered Office
3-6-272 Himayatnagar
Hyderabad 500 029 (A.P.), INDIA

Other Offices
CALCUTTA, MADRAS, MUMBAI, NEW DELHI
Bangalore, Bhubaneswar, Cochin, Guwahati, Hyderabad, Lucknow, Patna

© Orient Longman Limited, 1996
First Published 1996

ISBN 81 250 0364 9

Typeset by
Trans-Edit
B-11 Press Enclave
Saket, New Delhi 110 017

Printed in India at
Baba Barkha Nath Printers
26/7 Najafgarh Road Industrial Area
New Delhi 110 015

Published by
Orient Longman Limited
1/24 Asaf Ali Road
New Delhi 110 002

Contents

To
Chitra
my wife

whose relentless opposition to this entire project and uncompromising rejection of every salient point herein have dispelled any lingering doubt as to the need, the urgent need, for this book.

Preface

Ceylon? Why Ceylon and not Sri Lanka?

Ceylon? Why Ceylon and not Sri Lanka? Is it not regressive to hark back to a name redolent of colonial subjugation, anglicisation and cultural arrogance? It is. But no more so than the declared war-aim of the government of Sri Lanka which is the preservation of the "unitary state". The "unitary state" is an ambiguous phrase used at times in a geographical sense to mean one single state encompasssing the whole island and, at other times in a constitutional sense to mean a non-federal state with one supreme central government, whatever gradations of local government there may be. A unitary state in the former, territorial sense was established on the island on an enduring basis only under British colonial rule and under the name Ceylon. So that name helps take us to the heart of the present discord. In the war now being waged on the island one side aims to preserve the territorial integrity of that colonial construction, and the other side, to break it into two.

Prior to the establishment of the unitary state of Ceylon by the British, a variety of kingdoms co-existed side by side on the island. In both ancient and medieval periods there were brief episodes of a single kingdom under a Sinhala monarch covering the whole island but they were of short duration, lasting only for a part of that monarch's reign. No entities that even remotely resembled "states" in the current sense were then known. And multiplicity rather than unity was the norm. It was so even under Portuguese and Dutch colonial rule. The unitary state in both its geographical and constitutional senses is a purely British invention. It was established to satisfy colonial administrative convenience and made no pretence of being in response to the wishes, express or implied, of the governed. The British were well aware that two wholly disparate (and in the past frequently antagonistic) races were thus yoked together under their rule but administrative convenience was all that mattered.

The pattern of colonial rule in this respect was the same in Britain's other Asian colonies — India, Burma and the Malay peninsula. In all of them the impossibility of maintaining a "unitary state" became evident either at the point of decolonisation or soon thereafter. India split up immediately into India and Pakistan; shortly after independence the Malay peninsula divided into Malaysia, Singapore and Brunei; in Burma the tribal areas right round the border shook off Burmese rule and are still fighting for their independence. All these break-ups corresponded to the wishes of the people concerned — and the fissiparous trend continues. Pakistan divided into two — Bangladesh and Pakistan. India, despite its federal constitution, is threatened by several secessionist movements — in Jammu and Kashmir, in Assam, in the Punjab and in the tribal areas on the eastern border. And the tremors are being felt even in larger states like Tamilnadu.

Ceylon was the exception, initially, to this general trend. There was one vital reason for this. Ceylon gained its independence in 1948 not as a result of a people's mass movement (which was Gandhi's crucial contribution to the Indian independence movement) but by negotiation between the British establishment and a thoroughly anglicised local middle class elite comprising both Sinhala and Tamil professionals. It was on them that the imperial power devolved. It was their hope to step into the shoes of the departing British and run the country in the same benevolent style with the trappings of parliamentary government well under their paternalistic control. They counted without the hydra-headed monster of ethnic sub-nationalism which was soon to show how "the best-laid plans of mice and men gang aft agley"

1

The Psychology of Nationalism

The transition from a sense of community to a feeling of nationhood follows no set pattern. Nor is there any rule as to the sector of society from which the impetus towards nationhood emerges. The example of neighbouring peoples, the rising tide of prosperity and expectations, the ambition of a charismatic leader, alleged, perceived or real oppression — any of these may play a part and this is by no means an exhaustive list. While any of them or many in combination may serve as the catalyst, the basic material required for combustion is a common ethnic composition, a common language and culture, a common religion and the occupation of a contiguous land mass over a historical span of time.

The intensity of nationalistic feelings may vary from time to time according to changing circumstances. When an imperial hegemony is imposed, invariably by force of arms, national feelings run high. As imperial rule becomes settled, national consciousness lies low and dormant but unextinguished. As the grip of empire begins to weaken, rumblings of national independence, a reversion to indigenous cultures begin to manifest themselves. And the manner in which imperial rule ends, influences the course and intensity of nationalism. Where there is a mass movement for independence — the sort of movement that Gandhi led against British rule in India — the tide of nationalism runs very high indeed. There is invariably a renaissance of indigenous culture, a rejection of things and notions foreign and a conscious effort to recreate an idiosyncratic image. There is a great emotional surge; the adrenalin of independence revitalises society. It unleashes forces of human commitment and sacrifice that have overpowered academic doctrines and revolutionary ideologies. It is a force capable of destroying old orders and constructing new ones. And, historically, far from being a force that is spent it may only just be gathering momentum.

When Ceylon achieved its independence in 1948, however, a full-blown nationalistic mass uprising was absent. There was no parallel to the situation in neighbouring India which had achieved its goal just half a year earlier. Freedom came easily by friendly negotiation. There was little or no controversy over preservation of British investments, the continuance of British naval facilities and the adoption of British forms of parliamentary government including the first-past-the-post electoral system. The local elite who had settled the terms with the British came to power. And on an apparent sea of tranquillity sail was set to the fair winds of measured progress and steady "development". To the superficial observer the portents for success looked more promising than in most other colonies that the British were leaving.

The former colony of Ceylon became the new state of Ceylon. Indeed, the name lasted for the first 24 years of independence — that is more than half the period up to the time of the writing of this book. Nor was there any widespread demand for its change.

But was the new state a "nation-state"? Was there a "Ceylonese" nation on which it was grounded? The ambiguity and qualifications that must attach to any true answer to this question presaged the shoals that lay in the future. The middle class, both Sinhala and Tamil, perhaps 10 per cent of the population then, did feel they were "Ceylonese" but without any loss, of their ethnic identity as Sinhala or Tamil. Indeed, this writer, on his first trip abroad on government business in 1958, claimed he was a "Ceylonese" and so did his Tamil colleague who accompanied him. In the next, much larger stratum of the population — the lower middle class which was not wholly English-speaking — the Ceylonese identity, if it existed at all, was very weak indeed, barely vestigial. And for the vast majority of the population, of both races, the concept of a "Ceylonese" nationality was simply non-existent and unknown. Thus, to consider the new state of Ceylon a "nation-state" would be an exercise in optimism rather than reality. Ceylon was, and Sri Lanka continued to be, the former colonial contraption which in British times had been held together by force of British arms. With the disappearance of that "glue", things began to come unstuck.

Though a "Ceylonese" nation did not exist, nationalism was not absent. And from its very first manifestations, the divergence between the two races became apparent. Sinhala nationalism (which the Tamils were later to call "Sinhala chauvinism") arose from a Buddhist revival in the early years of this century and crystallised around the charismatic figure of Anagarika Dharmapala. The two movements were symbiotic and inextricable. And they found their home in the Sinhala lower middle class which had fared relatively badly under the British who favoured Tamils of the same social stratum for government jobs and other forms of preferment. This class had not been entirely culturally subverted by anglicisation as was the middle class and it was predominantly Buddhist. It arrived at the point of independence with an axe to grind against the Tamils. It looked to the Sinhala politicians, who had now come to power, to redress balance. It was a limited nationalism of a petit-bourgeois variety and it was based on a sense of self-interest that excluded the interests of the Tamils. It was ethnic nationalism, not the nationalism of a multi-ethnic unitary state.

Equally, there was a national upsurge on the Tamil side as well. Just prior to independence, when the constitution of the new state-to-be was being drafted by the Soulbury Commission which had been sent out by the British Government for the purpose, the Tamil Congress asked for 50:50 representation of the two races in the legislature on the ground that the Tamil people should have an equal status to the Sinhala people in the new state to be constituted from both these races, regardless of the weight of numbers. All Sinhala politicians and the whole mass of Sinhala people of all classes found this demand inexplicable and provocative because they failed to understand that the Tamil leaders regarded the new state as a composite entity made up of two equal races, irrespective of their size. The concept of rights irrespective of size is not one easy to comprehend even now when the world has become used to states of vastly different size acting as equals in the United Nations and other international fora. In 1946 this was completely incomprehensible to the whole Sinhala race and, regrettably, it seems to be so to this day. The point, however, is that from that early time the Tamil leaders projected a sense of Tamil nationalism which insisted on equal rights in every respect for the Tamil people (it was too early then to talk of a Tamil "nation") in the new state-to-be. On their side too it was an ethnic nationalism, not the nationalism of a multi-ethnic unitary state.

The politicians who came to power in 1948 were drawn exclusively from the English-speaking, highly anglicized middle class of both races. Most of them were professional men, well-acquainted with each other and endowed with basically liberal instincts. They had been elected in September 1947 in the euphoria of impending independence and left to themselves were very unlikely to do anything to rock the boat. But left to themselves they were not. In a matter of months they were engulfed by the high tides of their respective nationalisms and they set a pattern, which was to last to the present day, of responding to that impetus rather than curbing it.

Whatever little chance there may have been of a genuinely "Ceylonese" nationalism growing up in time was aborted almost at conception. The unitary state, freed from the strait-jacket of imperial order, became the battle-ground of competing nationalisms which convulse the country to this day.

2

The Fallibility of Governments

The end of the imperial rule and its succession by an independent national government is a historic watershed in a country's life. Those like this writer who were privileged to witness the event will never forget the sense of fulfilment and expectation it induced. There was a universal assumption that an independent national government, especially one elected by universal franchise, must sui generis be better for the governed in every respect than the imperial rule it replaced. The sobering thought that governments could be fallible was farthest from the public consciousness.

And, indeed, the record of successive governments of every political hue cannot be said to be an unrelieved display of fallibility. On the contrary, much good has been done. Faced with the need to make choices on account of limited resources and seemingly limitless needs, wise choices were made. And there was public support across the board, spanning the ethnic divide, for them.

The large investment in agriculture and irrigation has brought Sri Lanka to the brink of self-sufficiency in its staple food — rice — thus saving large foreign currency expenditures on its import. The next large investment was on education. It has resulted in a strikingly high degree of literacy which in turn has enabled important programmes such as family planning to be implemented very effectively and with great social and economic benefits. The third area — public health services, both curative and preventive — has also much to show for the heavy investments in it. A low rate of infant mortality, a high and rising life expectancy and the control of major diseases such as tuberculosis and malaria are but some of the benefits.

The choice to divert limited resources preponderantly to these three sectors inevitably meant less for other sectors of the economy. The effect was felt most where the physical infrastructure was concerned and that in turn had serious consequences for economic growth and growth in employment. The physical infrastructure failed lamentably to keep abreast of modern developments. Roads, railways, electricity generation and distribution, urban sewage disposal systems — all fell behind, delaying and limiting industrial and tourism development. In all these respects Sri Lanka which at independence was right up in the leading ranks of South East Asian countries is today many decades behind. And the visual impact of this decline is arresting. Everyone who makes the three-and-a-half-hour flight from Singapore to Colombo is rocked on arrival by the comparative decrepitude of the surroundings.

With the benefit of hindsight one could question the wisdom of endowing some sectors so heavily at the expense of others. Would not a more balanced dispersion of resources have been more effective? The pros and cons of that question could be argued interminably. The important point, however, was that at the time the strategy was widely accepted across the political and ethnic spectrum.

While the strategy did not lead to polemics, its implementation did. And in two major sectors of emphasis the polemics were inter-ethnic.

In agriculture and irrigation most of the investment was on the reclamation and re-settlement of jungle land in the dry zone of the island. This comprised the entire area in which the indigenous Tamil population lived and parts of the adjacent provinces occupied by Sinhala and Muslim people. In the re-settlement programme the predominant trend of population movement was of landless Sinhala people drawn from the densely populated south-western and central areas of Sri Lanka into the newly-opened-up areas. There were Tamil settlers too but in smaller numbers and none of them were re-settled in the Sinhala-occupied provinces. It was a population movement pregnant with discordant possibilities for the future even though the protests at the time by the Tamil leaders were relatively low-key.

In the area of education too problems arose with regard to attempts to even out opportunities between historically better-favoured and less-favoured areas. Due to the efforts of Christian missionaries, especially American ones, in the Tamil areas both the northern and eastern provinces had old-established, western-oriented educational institutions which gave these areas an advantage over the rural Sinhala heartland which had only a traditional, Buddhist-temple-based medieval system of education which was purely literary in content. As educational investments began to produce acute competition for the limited number of university places each year, the government attempted by an arcane device termed "standardisation" to artificially redress the balance. This was resented by the Tamil population to whom education, especially of the western-oriented type, was the key to personal economic advancement in an increasingly competitive context. Thus implementation even of the commonly agreed strategy proved divisive.

It was, however, in a quite different and far more sensitive sphere that the fallibility of all the governments that have held power in Sri Lanka since independence was lamentably demonstrated. That sphere was the relationship between the two ethnic elements which composed the new state. And trouble started in the very first year of independence — 1948.

In November of that year the government succeeded in passing through Parliament a law defining citizenship of the new state in very restrictive terms which straightaway excluded the Indian Tamil plantation worker population, then about a million people, from citizenship. It did so by casting upon those who desired to obtain citizenship by registration the onus of nearly impossible levels of proof of birth (from birth records) in Sri Lanka of earlier generations. The universally accepted norm of birth in a country entitling a person to apply for its citizenship was abandoned. One's father (and in some cases one's grandfather) had also to be born in the country to qualify. It was a draconian law, vigorously and eloquently opposed in parliament by the Indian Tamil plantation workers' representatives but rammed through by the Sinhala majority.

The Indian Tamil plantation worker population, all resident in company-owned tenements (called "lines") were the backbone of the only modern sector of agriculture in the country: the tea and rubber plantations. They had been imported into Ceylon by the British to establish and operate the plantations as indigenous Sinhala rural people were engaged in their traditional subsistence agriculture and showed no inclination for abandoning its relaxed cycles of work and rest for the rigid regimentation of plantation agriculture under English superintendents. In 1931 when universal franchise (subject to the age of majority, then 21 years for both male and female) was introduced under British colonial rule, the Indian Tamil plantation worker population became entitled to the vote. They elected their own representatives wherever they were in a majority in an electorate at general elections in 1931 and 1936 to the then legislature, the State Council, and in 1947 to the newly-established parliament. They were a stable, law-abiding and economically vitally productive element of the population.

Without any provocation on their part and for no immediately visible reason the new law made them "stateless persons" overnight. The Sinhala and indigenous Tamil populations (the latter in the northern and eastern provinces of the island) became citizens by descent on the prima facie evidence of just their names. To make a million persons stateless in one fell swoop is a very serious matter, and the question arises immediately — what was the purpose of such an ugly discrimination where none had existed before? The answer was not long in coming. By another law introduced and passed early in 1949, voting rights at both parliamentary and local government elections were restricted to citizens under the 1948 law. The million persons having first been made stateless were immediately thereafter made voteless as well.

The psychological effect of being made both stateless and voteless is not known to any Sinhala or indigenous Tamil resident of the island. The persons so affected had leaders in the very parliament that perpetrated these iniquities. These representatives inveighed against them with all the force of reason, argument and eloquence they could muster. But the indigenous Tamil MPs, whose constituents were not affected by these laws, joined their Sinhala colleagues in passing these laws. However, two of their number broke ranks, joined the Indian Tamil MPs and opposed the majority, roundly condemning the laws and their effects. The Sinhala majority in Parliament, however, carried the day, and also succeeded in resisting an appeal to the Judicial Committee of the British Privy Council which held that defining its own citizenship within the country was a matter within the sole competence of a government of a country.

The right to define citizenship does not confer an absolute freedom to do so in ways harmful to large numbers of people. If the majority was so minded, the voting rights law could well have contained an exemption for the hundreds of thousands of persons who had enjoyed voting rights under British colonial rule. The fact that one law led to the other is reasonable ground for concluding that the one was the reason for the other.

It is interesting that during the months in which these two laws were proposed and discussed in Parliament not a single Sinhala voice was heard even to inquire what the affected people thought of the whole business, what their feelings were. In the much vaunted Sinhala moral ethos, hospitality and magnanimity to strangers in their midst is a hallmark tradition. That great virtue was notably absent then. It was a time when this writer was well able to judge the rights and wrongs of such an issue. But in him too no "still small voice of conscience" stirred.

The reasons are not far to seek. It was the universal attitude of Sinhala people that the new government was for their exclusive benefit, that these draconian laws against another people would somehow redound to their (the Sinhala people's) advantage and that the new government was acting both legitimately and in the best interests of those whom it represented. Little did they imagine how right they were — that it is the ethnic imperative that inspires governments in the newly-independent context. Those first months of independence set the stage for a Greek tragedy: the inexorable denouement is unfolding before our very eyes today.

The two indigenous Tamil MPs who broke with their colleagues and voted against the laws — Chelvanayakam and Vanniasingham — could see the writing on the wall for the indigenous Tamil people as well and said as much. They went on to found the Federal Party.

These events of the first year of independence are discussed at such length above because of their central importance for what was to follow. In the demarcation of electorates for the second general election — that of 1952 — the now disenfranchised Indian Tamil plantation workers were counted in the figure of 75,000 adults per electorate even though they had no votes. Those electorates had, in effect, only around 25,000 voters — all Sinhala — and this considerably increased the number of Sinhala MPs in the total. It was a form of gerrymandering that facilitated the passage of even more virulently pro-Sinhala legislation in succeeding years.

Thereafter, nationalistic fervour on both sides of the ethnic divide began to take firm hold. Not only politicians but the entire populations of the two races now became involved, and with that the stakes went up even higher. The two Sinhala political parties, the United National Party (UNP) and the Sri Lanka Freedom Party (SLFP) began bidding for the support of the most extreme nationalist elements in Sinhala society. The SLFP seized on the language issue and offered to replace English with "Sinhala only" as the sole official language of the country within 24 hours of it being voted into office. The UNP too then adopted the "Sinhala only" policy of the SLFP. The Federal Party asked for a constitutional change to a federal state with the northern and eastern provinces to be a single state of such a federation. All the Sinhala leaders opposed this with one voice — even the small Sinhala Marxist parties swept along by the tide of nationalism.

The general election of 1956 was fought in this heated atmosphere and resulted in overwhelming victories for the SLFP in the Sinhala areas and the Federal Party in the Tamil areas. The "Sinhala only" language legislation was passed as promised, followed by a pretense of "Tamil also" to appease the Tamils but the implementation of that was stifled by bureaucratic obstruction. The Federal Party continued its demand for a federal state in the context of rising inter-ethnic violence. The two sides then reached an agreement on a devolution of powers to a local assembly, only to have the Sinhala leaders withdraw from it on the ground that they could not carry it with their supporters.

From the story thus unfolding it would appear that the early governments after independence were bent on nothing short of self-destruction. Cynics observing the business of government have concluded acidly that most government activity produces the opposite of the intended result. In this case, however, the path to self-destruction is less oblique — the Gadarene slope to perdition is descended with loud hurrahs of discord all the way.

3

The Discouragement of Dissent : The Media

"Multi-party democracy" is these days a fervently desired objective, almost an end in itself, for Eastern European countries unshackling themselves from the communist strait-jacket and also for many countries in Africa. It is a sobering thought then that in a country in which it has existed untrammelled for 48 years, all is far from well. From the last years of colonial rule in Ceylon and since independence in 1948 there have been no restrictions on the formation of political parties. They cover the entire ideological spectrum from extreme right-wing religio-ethnic obscurantism through capitalism paying the obligatory lip-service to "socialism", feudal socialism, rampant populism and text-book Marxism right out to the outer fringes of the permanent revolution, Maoism, nihilism and anarchism.

These parties are, moreover, free to propound their creeds in speech and print. Only the libel laws act as a restraint and even they are skirted around with great adroitness. The legislature has always had an officially recognised opposition on the lines of Westminster and the steady, often virulent, criticism of the government in parliament is freely reported in the press and followed by a large reading public. The freedom of political debate in parliament is often claimed to be the final and conclusive proof of the existence and flourishing of a democratic order.

It cannot be denied that these are vital elements of the democratic process. But they are not the only elements and, perhaps, not even the most important. There are other essential aspects of attitude and conduct in the public domain, which though less tangible, are the key elements of a democratic climate and it is they, even more than the political posturings, that enable the undoubted blessings of democracy to be garnered for a people.

When all is said and done, political parties are only a small fraction of the population. The card-carrying, paid-up membership of all the political parties in the country put together is only a minuscule part of the total population. The public is a much larger body than the political parties and issues of public morality, the commitment of a whole people to right or wrong courses of action and especially to war, are matters that can seldom be left to politicians and political parties. The public at large has a vital stake in the quality and exercise of democratic life. And it is here that misgiving gives way to despair.

It is paradoxical that in a country with so much ideological debate there is hardly any discussion, public or private, of questions of public or national morality. And this is even more surprising at a time of war when young men are called to arms, licensed to kill an enemy and urged to give their lives for a cause. These are matters of life and death, not of political ideology or expediency. In countries in which democracy is a more personal, vibrant reality the questioning of war-aims is an important part of public life. During the Vietnam war anti-war protests spread across the whole spectrum of public life in the USA and eventually overwhelmed both political parties, the military-industrial complex and the US government. Contrariwise, an entire people is dragged into war for lack of public participation in the discussion of the rights or wrongs of what is being done by their government in their name. The most striking example, within the living memory of many people, is how for lack of such questioning, the German people found themselves in the hands of fascist thugs who railroaded them into war and disaster. The people of Iraq are today's exemplar of that pattern.

Sri Lanka today provides another illuminating example of what happens when the climate of freedom necessary for the expression of a wide variety of opinions outside the field of politics and political parties is absent. Fundamental questions as to the merits of, and the cost of preserving, the unitary state, that is, a single state encompassing the whole island, are taboo. Equally fundamental questions of the value of a unitary state as against a federal one are out of bounds. Even more fundamental questions as to the morality of killing and being killed over constitutional and geo-political issues are not even asked, let alone answered. These are not just matters for political debate — they are questions of public morality and they impinge on the moral integrity of every individual who makes up that "public".

Not only is the open discussion of such matters frowned upon by the politicians and the government, the very constitution of the country has been amended to foreclose even the possibility of public debate on the division of the island into two states as a viable course to peace. There can be very few constitutions in the world which impose such a barrier to freedom of public expression and discussion on the people governed by them. And such an absurdity is counter-productive — as in the instant case. Not only did it lead immediately to the departure of the Tamil MPs of the Tamil United Liberation Front (TULF) from Parliament thus rendering it an unrepresentative rump, it did far worse damage to the Sinhala people by putting beyond their reach a possible path to peace. All the Sinhala political parties supported, and still support, this legislative monstrosity which is so manifestly injurious to the very people whom they are supposed to represent.

At the practical, pragmatic level too, subtle forms of brainwashing inhibit the free expression of opinion. Any independent view as to the ability of a paid professional army to win a guerilla war is squelched as traitorous and unpatriotic. A calm, dispassionate, public discussion of the lessons to be learnt from recent military history in comparable contexts is impossible. The assumption of inevitable victory in this conflict of arms is placed as much beyond question as it was for the people of Iraq by their government just before the Gulf war proved how hollow such brainwashing is.

Even worse, the public is fed biased information bolstered by bi-partisan support from the Sinhala political parties affirming endlessly the justice of the Sinhala cause in the conflict and the need to support a freely elected government's efforts to "save the country". The experience of other countries, some very closely linked to Sri Lanka, which point the other way is never mentioned. It is not part of the public consciousness and of public knowledge in Sri Lanka today that Great Britain had its own "Eelam question"; that the once-unitary state of Great Britain and Ireland which encompassed the whole of the British Isles was split, after a long-drawn out conflict with Irish nationalism, into two independent, sovereign states in 1922 — the one a monarchy (the kingdom of Great Britain and Northern Ireland) and the other a republic (the Irish Free State now The Republic of Ireland). The mother country of the then

greatest empire in the world, one of the most advanced industrial
countries of that time, could not preserve its own territorial integrity in the face of a nationalist uprising in its midst. And it was not
for want of trying.

Nor is any mention made in public discussion of another country
which too had former colonial links with Ceylon — the Netherlands. There three neighbouring countries, all independent monar-
chies with governments, armies and currencies of their own, and
occupying a land area which in total is only a few square miles more
than the land area of the island of Ceylon, joined in a union — the
Benelux Union — which was the forerunner of the European
Community. The Benelux Union enables the subjects of one country
to live freely in either of the others; it has abolished all trade and
customs barriers between the three countries which live in peace
and harmony with each other despite great differences of language,
religion and culture.

All these and many more are perfectly viable options open to the
Sinhala people. But they are brainwashed into believing that fighting to preserve the "unitary state" is the only option available to
them. A dispassionate, informed, humane public discussion of
other possible alternatives is totally precluded. How is it that a
literate, deeply religious and generally peaceable people such as the
Sinhala people can be brought to such a pass?

The fundamental cause is the political manipulation of rising
national sentiment among the Sinhala people. There has been a
symbiotic relationship between politics and nationalism — each
has fed upon the other. Politicians of all parties have acquired a sixth
sense to judge which national issue would be likely to catch the
prevailing wind at any given time — sometimes race (vide chapter
2), sometimes religion, sometimes language. When one set of
politicians seizes upon some such "trump card", all the others
follow suit to avoid isolation and unpopularity. The depths of
absurdity were plumbed by one party even using its tenure in
power to abandon the weeks of the Gregorian calendar in favour of
"weeks" of uneven length determined by the phases of the moon
according to which Buddhist religious observance goes. Any opposing voice ran the risk of being branded as traitorous to the
national cause. This demonising of dissent led to the narrowing of
choices in public thinking and finally railroaded society into toeing
the "party line"

The freedom to consider a wide range of options, the freedom to question the received wisdom, the freedom to look directly and objectively at sacred cows, the freedom to express dissent and to canvass support for it, the freedom always to judge the morality and humanity of every action of government all go to form a climate of public life in which the practice (as opposed to the preaching) of democracy can flourish. All these barely saw the light of day in independent Ceylon, still less in later Sri Lanka.

There was, and is, an expressed rationale in favour of conformity in public opinion on the central issues of national identity and against any dissent on them. The argument runs thus — in a newly-independent developing country the government had to take the leading role in all aspects of national life. For that it needed solid, cohesive public backing for its basic policies. Open dissent would weaken the state — unity was strength. Thus was the essence of democratic life stood upon its head. With it the flood-gates of political and official abuse and corruption were opened and the arena of government became the happy hunting ground of politicians "on the make". Worse still, when the argument was applied to preserving a political system and culture derived from a colonial past it totally alienated the rising rural intelligentsia produced by the free education policy and led to the successive civil wars of 1971 and the eighties waged by the Janatha Vimukthi Peramuna (JVP).

If democracy is ever to come alive in the country there has to be a complete U-turn in respect of the toleration of dissent even on the most fundamental issues. The academic analysis of dissentient views must be encouraged. The experiences of all countries which are relevant to the situation in Sri Lanka must be dispassionately considered and made available to the public. There must be a widening rather than a narrowing of choices. The Sinhala people have been backed into a corner and told war is the only way out. That is the fallacy that must be stood upon its head.

All of the foregoing point to a malaise in every aspect of the media — the press, radio and television. In the older democratic countries the media perform a vital "public-interest" service by both expressing its own independent views on important matters in national life and also providing a forum for a wide range of opinions. This pattern was set by the press and was followed by radio and TV. Due to its vital importance for the effective functioning of democracy the freedom of the media now receives bi-partisan support in the western liberal democracies. The media influence the quality of democratic action in public life and the course of parliamentary government. It is hyper-sensitive to issues of war and peace and strains to dredge up every shade of dissenting opinion, good, bad and indifferent at such times. This concept of the media's public duty was magnificently demonstrated in Britain during the recent Gulf war.

In colonial times the English language press in Ceylon had a great deal of freedom and used it to good effect in respect of the progressive reform of the constitution and the movement towards independence. With the arrival of independence these very newspapers accepted the newly-independent government's view that it needed public support across the board for the work of national regeneration. The press accordingly set about orchestrating public support for the government quite uncritically. The close links of family and familiarity between the press owners of that time and the new ruling elite facilitated this transition to the new concept of public service by the press. This is why in the very first year of independence (1948) when the fateful legislation on citizenship was passed, the press did not rock the boat. Not only did the English language newspapers (then the most influential in the country) fail to point out the iniquity and latent dangers of those laws, it also failed to bring to public attention the cogent criticisms of those laws by the affected parties and others concerned — the leaders of the Tamil plantation workers and the apprehensive leaders of the indigenous Tamil people respectively. A great opportunity for building a solid democratic foundation for the newly-independent state was wasted. The practice of unquestioning support for the government soon degenerated into appalling sycophancy and the loss of public confidence and respect. Thereafter, fitful attempts at journalistic independence within the existing newspapers or by the establishment of new titles were quickly suppressed by official brow-beating or closure without compensation or nationalisation. There was, and is, bipartisan support for this attitude towards a free press. Anyone who comes to Sri Lanka from neighbouring India with its sturdily independent English language press or from Singapore or Hongkong with their world-class dailies will see and feel instantly the extent of the disaster. Not only are the English language newspapers in Sri Lanka ill-written and ill-printed, their quality as vehicles of enlightened, modern, humane opinion is abysmal. They promote the climate of unquestioning conformity which is so dangerous to a people ever more deeply embroiled in war.

As went the press so also went radio and TV — only more so as they were directly set up and owned by the government. The obligatory lip-service to democracy is paid by the "equal time" provision for political parties during elections. But no independence in the analysis of news or policies or in comment thereon is allowed or attempted. These vital ingredients of democratic life have been co-opted wholesale into the government. All that is necessary for railroading public opinion and the public into courses chosen by politicians is at hand without their being exposed to a wide variety of informed and dissenting views and opinions, especially on the issues of war and peace.

4

The Panacea of Democracy

"A little knowledge is a dangerous thing
Drink deep or drink not of the Pierian spring"

These lines of Alexander Pope come forcefully to mind whenever the government of Sri Lanka lays claim to its democratic credentials. And the claim is made at every turn. It is used in soliciting aid from donor countries; it is used to drum up support for the war; it is used to berate those who dare oppose the government; it is used in demonising the LTTE and its claim for a separate state.

This assertion of democratic virtue is based on the assumption that a constitution which requires regular national elections, the formation of the legislature and the executive from representatives elected at such elections (and since 1978 the direct election, by a national constituency, of the president who is the head of the executive), and changes in both according to electoral fortune are, taken together, a sufficient guarantee of democratic order in society. It is assumed that a government elected under these undoubtedly democratic arrangements must ipso facto be itself democratic in nature. There is the underlying suggestion that whatever such a government does, not only has democratic legitimacy but is also beneficial to the governed.

All governments in Sri Lanka during the last 48 years of independence have the same democratic credentials. They have been elected to, and turned out of, office by the will of the people expressed at general elections. However, the democratic election of governments has not ensured democratic governance. As explained in Chapter 2, the very first government elected in 1947, just prior to all, since it was elected on genuine universal suffrage with the Tamil plantation workers voting, besmirched the statute book with manifestly undemocratic legislation. Succeeding governments (elected since the second general election — that of 1952 — on a restricted franchise which excluded the Tamil plantation worker population right up to 1988) did even worse. The period of "democratic" government since independence has seen two extremely bloody civil wars among the Sinhala people and an eight-year-long still-running guerilla war with the Tamil secessionist movement; not to mention numerous inter-ethnic clashes, bloodshed and loss of civilian lives from 1956 to 1983 i.e. for 27 out of the 48 years of independence. All governments which have faced these challenges have stigmatised their opponents as "anti-democratic". The undemocratic legislation of the governments themselves has seldom been acknowledged as being no small part of the cause of these disasters.

From mid-1987 onwards the undemocratic legislation referred to in the earlier chapters has been reversed by corrective laws. Citizenship has been conferred on the Tamil plantation worker population; voting rights have been restored to them; language discrimination has been ended. These changes came about not by a democratic acknowledgement of the wrongs done by earlier "democratic" governments but by way of offers for a settlement of the guerilla war with the indigenous Tamils. They were the result of a presidential volte face in 1987 against the wishes of the then Parliament (which was later browbeaten into compliance) and of all the Sinhala political parties including his own. It is war that has purged the statute book of iniquity, not democratic virtue. Thirty five years of unremitting effort in the democratic arena by the elected representatives of the indigenous Tamil people produced nothing; it is only unrelenting guerilla warfare that has forced these salutary changes upon the Sinhala government. It is supremely ironic that 48 years of "democratic" government have established the necessity of war to secure equity.

It is a legitimate question whether a form of government other than democracy — say autocracy either civil or military — might have averted these disasters. Forms of societal organisation have to be judged not by their claims to virtue but by their results and democracy is not exempt from that test. Certainly life under colonial rule in the last years under the British was far less bloody and far more democratic as all residents of voting age had the vote. There was universal suffrage then — and after a 40-year lapse Sri Lanka is just returning to it now. British colonial rule even today in Hongkong is incomparably more beneficial to the governed than the rule of most newly-independent ex-colonial states. The record of a military autocracy in Indonesia for the last many years is no mean achievement, for it has provided the large population of that country with a reasonable tranquillity and striking improvements in every area of public well-being.

So, has democracy failed in Sri Lanka? The answer must surely be "No" for the simple reason that democracy has not been tried. What has been tried in the name of democracy is a mechanistic form of political organisation, producing an institution to succeed the imperial power. Democracy is not a political structure; it is a concept of society from which spring institutions of various types — government is but one of them — to give effect to society's democratic aspirations. A democratic society and a democratically elected government need to be in a symbiotic relationship, and mutually nourish each other. The latter without the former is but a travesty of the whole concept.

The attempt to have a democratic government which is not grounded in a democratic social order leads unsurprisingly to the results seen in Sri Lanka. The basic concept of democracy needs to be revised and re-understood and this is a process now going on worldwide. That is how the primacy of human rights vaulting the barriers of sovereignty and committing people across the world to each other's peace and welfare irrespective of state boundaries has come about.

The concept of human rights is, perhaps, the most significant ideological development of the second half of this century. While the first half was dominated by the communist and socialist ideologies and the varying political expressions thereof, the concept of human rights has emerged as the ideological groundwork of the liberal democracies. The concept is not a static one confined to the Universal Declaration of Human Rights of 1948 — it is a dynamic one based on the constant application of humane and ethical considerations to varying contexts and developments.

The primacy of the individual, the sanctity of human life, the duty of society to ensure for the individual the opportunity for a good life consonant with the same opportunity for others, the subordination of political concepts such as sovereignty or national security to human rights are all now gaining widespread acceptance. Where due process of law is denied or is absent, the defence of sovereign right or national security is no longer deemed sufficient. The universality of the concept of human rights increasingly warrants international intervention in intra-national disputes. The tieing of multi-lateral and bi-lateral aid to verifiable human rights norms is now common and is becoming entrenched in the domestic legislation of many donor countries. The UN itself is beginning to see a role for itself in interventionist activity in cases of dire oppression of a national minority.

The assumption of sovereign status by a people with a national identity and in historical occupation of a territory is today a part of the growing panoply of human rights. In former times such a situation led to long-running civil war and eventual secession (e.g. Eire from Great Britain or Eritrea from Ethiopia) or foreign intervention (e.g. Bangladesh from Pakistan). A combination of civil war and foreign compassionate intervention has already launched Slovenia and Croatia into international orbit and others of the former constituent republics of the federation of Yugoslavia may soon follow. The dissolution of the Soviet Union into independent ethnic states either related to each other in a loose commonwealth or totally independent as in the case of the Baltic states is but the latest example. The fulfilment of a people's national aspiration for statehood and independence is not today a ground for war and sacrifice of human life.

In the post-World War II period decolonization process, the right to independent statehood even for the entities insensitively cobbled together by the imperial powers was widely recognized. In many of these newly-independent states, the fissiparous tendencies are now becoming open and visible. If self-determination was good at the point of decolonization why is it bad later? The denial of claims to independent statehood raises questions not only of military capability (i.e. whether the movement for independence can be crushed militarily or whether neighbouring states should succour those who fight for their freedom and independence) but also even weightier questions of public morality such as on which side lies the balance of right and wrong.

What should be the democratic course in such a situation? Is vox populi also vox dei? Can a democratic society handle such a demand? In Great Britain there was a referendum on Scottish secession. In Canada the secession of Quebec from the federation is at the forefront of current political debate. The last constitution of the Soviet Union provided explicitly for secession. Secession is a matter capable of democratic resolution in a democratic society. And the basic grounding of such a resolution must be the common recognition that human life is more important than political or geographical structures. States and state structures are the handiwork of man and there is nothing irrevocable about them. There is nothing sacrosanct about the state, be it unitary or otherwise. Man on the other hand is of God and human life is not to be weighed in the same balance with political expediency or political structures. A "democracy" which is not founded upon such a commonly held consensus can easily be sucked into war unthinkingly — and of such a society and such a situation Sri Lanka today is a classic example. Only a new comprehension of democracy and of human rights can now pave the way to peace.

5

The Legacy of the Constitutional Pundits

In this chapter the term "unitary state" is used not in its geographic connotation (i.e. one state encompassing the whole island) but in its constitutional sense to mean a centrally governed state as opposed to a federally organised one.

The colonial experience entailed many novel departures for both Sinhala and Tamil peoples. One of the more significant was their first encounter with the concept and practice of a modern state based on the rule of law. Nothing in the previous history of both peoples even remotely resembled the form of government to which they were subjected, especially by the British. The medieval concepts and practices of a feudal, service-based relationship to an individual ruler were replaced by the equality of individuals before the law and private rights to "life, liberty and the pursuit of happiness" Even though it came under the aegis of an imperial master, the impact of the modern state was very penetrating and the eventual attribution of virtual sanctity to it is not surprising. Today the desire for a state of ones's own is so strong it has impelled the Tamil people to take up arms and willingly sacrifice their lives to secure one for themselves. A state is regarded as an essential attribute of nationhood and the means by which a nation's sovereignty and independence is expressed and safeguarded.

In European cultures, on the other hand, there is a high degree of ambivalence about the importance of the state. For many centuries the church had supremacy over the state and the state itself evolved towards its modern form by slow stages. Even in its modern form the sanctity of the state, its exercise of sovereignty and other attributes of state power are subjected to a constant questioning. The state is regarded not as an end in itself but as a means of securing the safety and well-being of the society in which it is grounded. In the western liberal democracies, especially in the European community, the inadequacy of existing nation-states in serving these ends in the face of competition from super-powers, especially economic super-powers, is leading to the erosion of the autonomy of the nation-state and to the rise of various forms of association better suited to serving their people's needs. The struggle of the Tamil people to establish a new nation-state for themselves is somewhat anachronistic in this day and age. But, perhaps, the nation-state is an essential way-station on the road to eventual free association — and "free" is the key word, for any form of association for mutual benefit has to be free and voluntary and not imposed, least of all by force.

In Sri Lanka there is no tradition of questioning the purposes and usefulness of the state. The unitary state bequeathed by the departing imperial power was regarded as the most essential part of society. But it contained a fatal flaw — it was not a state based upon a nation; it was a state superimposed upon two nations by an imperial power. Despite this, however, the successor state sought to continue as before, a unitary state. The only difference was one of emphasis not character — the role of government was to be expanded in the interests of development. The example of the neighbouring newly-independent state, India, changing from unitary to federal form at independence had no impact in Sri Lanka. In the latter the unitary form was considered essential for the strong executive needed for rapid development.

This concept was powerfully re-inforced by the first of the constitutional pundits to play a role — William Ivor Jennings, the first Vice-Chancellor of the newly-created (1942) University of Ceylon. He was then the leading authority on cabinet government in Britain and soon became a trusted confidante of the man who was to become the first prime minister of the newly-independent country, Don Stephen Senanayake. In the preparation of the new constitution (which was to be passed by an Act of the British Parliament) Ivor Jennings played a vital role. He provided for a bi-cameral legislature and a cabinet form of executive based on political parties and their representation in Parliament. He aimed to establish a Westminster type of government but with the difference that it was to be based upon a written constitution (in Britain there was, and still is, no written constitution).

However, while Jennings was influential in the matter of constitutional form, the models followed in the actual business of government came from elsewhere. The Soviet and Indian practice of 5-year plans, implementation programmes etc. were adopted as essential to good government and development. International institutions such as the IMF and World Bank encouraged this trend. Thus the Westminster system, based on annual budgets and flexible enough to adapt to fast changing conditions, was pressed into service amidst the alien rigidities of long-, mid-, and short-term planning.

The next lot of constitutional pundits to come on the scene had a less benign influence than Jennings. The Trotskyist leaders, N.M. Perera and Colvin R. de Silva were, paradoxically, steeped in constitutional theory and practice in the western liberal democracies. Both had been at the London School of Economics over which Harold Laski had held sway and N.M. Perera had collaborated with Herman Finer in his monumental *Theory and Practice of Modern Governments* which became a sort of Bible for students of politics in the forties. Though not in government in the early years of independence they wielded a disproportionate degree of influence from the opposition benches in Parliament on account of their academic eminence (both had doctorates from the LSE) and skill in debate. They advanced the concept not only of government intervention in the economy to regulate market forces but also of the curbing of market forces by a great panoply of government controls. This led eventually to direct entry by government into business and the creation of monopolies for some such businesses on various pretexts. President Calvin Coolidge is reported to have said with his legendary terseness that "the business of business is business". Our pundits were not far from the proposition that the business of government was business!

Thus came into being an array of public sector businesses which soon overshadowed the private sector. Finally, plantations over 50 acres in extent were nationalised by the use of foreign aid (to pay off British plantation owners) in 1975. With that the state became supreme in society. It controlled not merely the "commanding heights of the economy" but it marched over its length and breadth as well. State business enterprises were called "corporations" in a curious inversion of meaning similar to the term "public school" in England. Except for a handful of these corporations which were given a monopoly over their respective areas of business, the majority of the rest made, and continue to make losses which are made good by tax revenues. The cost to the tax-payer has never been, and perhaps never will be, counted. Appointments to lucrative positions on the boards of directors of these corporations with all the attendant perks of official cars and chauffeurs etc. as well as employment at all levels within them is entirely in the hands of cabinet ministers. The whole area of public sector corporations is one of patronage and favours to be given and received, giving rise to a new privileged class which is hand in glove with politicians of all parties.

The relaxation of government controls since 1977 and relative non-intervention in market forces has not gone as far as a fundamental revision of constitutional philosophy regarding the role of the state vis-a-vis the market. The "mixed-economy" continues with the profits of private sector businesses being siphoned away by taxation to subsidise loss-making sacred cows — the corporations. The capital so sorely needed for the enormous investment required to modernise the infrastucture is sacrificed to a massive political pay off via the corporations.

The "radicalism" that led to state intervention and participation in the business sector, however, did not extend to dealing with the far more urgent questions raised by national cohabitations — the strains and stresses arising from two nations living cheek by jowl with each other within the constraints of a single constitutional framework. The first manifestation of trouble came early. The demand for a federal constitution goes back to 1948 — the very year of independence when Messrs Chelvanayakam and Vanniasingham quit the Tamil Congress in protest against the first anti-democratic, ethnically discriminatory legislation of the newly elected government.

Admittedly there was no experience of the federal form of government in Sri Lanka but many of the larger members of the Commonwealth were federal states — Australia, Canada, India. There was a facile conclusion that federal constitutions were suitable only for large states overlooking the case of a far smaller country than Sri Lanka — Switzerland — which was a successful federal state. Moreover, both India and Switzerland were federations of ethnic states, a condition applicable to the Sri Lankan situation. The logic of a federal constitution for an ethnic state federation in Sri Lanka is so obvious that its virtual ostracism from public debate and eventual demonizing should be examined at length.

Inter-ethnic hostility was such that any Tamil demand, especially one that gave them equality of status as a component part of a federal state, was rejected out of hand. The very word "federal" raised the hackles of Sinhala politicians. The mere discussion of federalism as a possible option was regarded among Sinhala people as unpatriotic. Any talk of a federal constitution was banished from the public domain as far as Sinhala people were concerned. And this played directly into the hands of the younger, aggressive Tamil nationalists in whose interests it was to point to the unreasonableness of Sinhala governments and the futility of seeking a federal solution. From that it was but a short step to the assertion that the Tamils had no hope of equity by democratic or constitutional means within the existing unitary state. And at every turn the worst predictions of the rising young (and increasingly militant) Tamil nationalists were fulfilled with unerring insensitivity by successive Sinhala governments. Indeed it is not too far-fetched to say that in a very real sense Mr. Prabhakaran is the creature of the ignorance and mindless intransigence of the Sinhala governments.

While the demand of the moderate Tamil politicians for a federal constitution was thus being rejected out of hand without any dispassionate public discussion of its merits or demerits, the constitutional pundits, Messrs Perera and de Silva, now entrenched in power as ministers in Mrs. Bandaranaike's last government, busied themselves with the making of a new constitution. In 1972 it was adopted and Sri Lanka became a "socialist republic" shedding its historic monarchical carapace. The legislature was changed from bicameral to unicameral and the very name of the country, Ceylon, an anglicization of earlier Portuguese (Ceilao) and Dutch (Zeylan) names was replaced by the purely Sinhala name, Sri Lanka. This was the high-watermark of ethnic insensitiveness and predictably the elected representatives of the Tamil people boycotted the constituent assembly which wrought these changes.

The preamble to this constitution contained a portentious piece of rhetoric (de Silva was justly renowned for his rhetoric in Parliament, on political platforms and in the law courts — he was a leading criminal lawyer) with incalculable consequences for the future. It declared that the "sovereign people of Sri Lanka give unto themselves this constitution". The implications were clear — a people had a right to assume sovereignty and, having done so, to exercise it by adopting a constitution for their country. It was accepted as divine truth that the Sinhala people, even without the consent of the elected representatives of the Tamil people, had a right to act in this way. Can it then be rationally claimed that only the Sinhala people and no other people have such a right?

The object of the constitution of the First Republic (1972) was to break ostentatiously with the colonial past, not to deal with the rancorous ethnic discord that plagued the country. It was as vainglorious a form of posturing as Nero fiddling while Rome burnt. Such is the hollowness of the legacy of the constitutional pundits, a legacy which hastened the day of eventual reckoning.

6

The Turning Point — The General Election of 1977

One of the claims made for the democratic nature of politics in Ceylon is that governments have been changed at general elections at regular intervals since 1956. Six such changes have taken place — first in 1956, then twice in 1960, in 1965, in 1970 and finally in 1977. It is tempting to say that those changes were effected peacefully through the ballot rather than the bullet but the fact of the matter is that each successive general election witnessed a rising crescendo of violence and killings. And the general election of 1977 was no exception in this respect.

It was, however, a great turning point in the history of the country for many important reasons. And they may be classified under two heads.

The first was the radical new right-wing agenda of the UNP. It aimed at rescuing the country from the morass of stagnation, unemployment and general decrepitude brought about by seven continuous years of socialist government under the SLFP-LSSP coalition (which itself broke up towards the end of this period). The chaos resulting from a centrally-planned economy administered by a vast array of controls with government itself monopolising large areas of economic life was first demonstrated in Sri Lanka. The examples of Cuba, the former Soviet Union and other such states reinforce the inevitability of the tragic results of this type of government.

The UNP promised to dismantle the controls and liberalize imports. Exchange controls were to be relaxed and far-reaching incentives were to be offered for foreign investment. The food rationing system was to be replaced by social security measures based on means tests and there was to be a return to free markets.

Equally significant were the UNP's offers of constitutional reform. For the first time in any Asian democracy an elected executive presidency on French lines was proposed and even more significantly the British "first-past-the-post" electoral system was to be replaced by proportional representation on European lines. These were unique departures from the British political culture which was part of the inherited baggage of colonial rule.

Never before or since has the electorate been offered such sweeping changes in both economic and constitutional areas of the body politic. It was right-wing radicalism at its most innovative and constructive — light years ahead of the tired and confused socialist nostrums of Mrs. Bandaranaike's last years in office.

The second set of reasons was even more important than the first though it was well shielded from public perception. To understand it in its true perspective it is necessary briefly to recount the background.

The Federal Party had been founded in 1948 to secure for the indigenous Tamil people of Ceylon a Tamil state which would be one of the federating units in a federal state. As mentioned in the preceding chapter the Sinhala reaction was to exclude the very word "federal" from the language of political discourse. Nevertheless, attempts were made to accord to the Tamil people in the northern and eastern provinces some degree of local autonomy short of federal status. The Bandaranaike-Chelvanayakam pact and the Dudley Senanayake-Chelvanayakam Agreement were the results of these efforts. Both were aborted almost at birth as the Sinhala leader in each case was unable to secure the support of the Sinhala MPs to carry through the necessary legislation in Parliament.

The Federal Party was led by lawyers who believed in lawful, constitutional means for securing what seemed to them an arrangement which was both rational and necessary if serious trouble was to be avoided. They were beginning to feel the discontent and turbulence within the ranks of their younger members. The fires of nationalism were kindling among them and the Federal Party hoped to avert a conflagration by timely action. With every failure it encountered, however, scepticism about its leadership began to grow and hope began to fade as to the efficacy of peaceful constitutional action in securing Tamil aspirations.

These aspirations themselves took a quantum leap as the federal ideal faded. The concept of an independent Tamil state began to grow and take hold among large sections of Tamil youth in the northern and eastern provinces. A host of militant groups appeared with varying ideological agendas as to the nature and political philosophy of the future Tamil state but all were agreed on the need for one as an essential attribute of the Tamil nation.

It is these groups that formed the "Front" — a classic revolutionary term — along with the fast-fading Federal Party to fight the 1977 general election. The Tamil United Liberation Front (TULF) as it was called had, as the first point of its election manifesto the promise "to secure, if possible by constitutional and peaceful means, a separate, independent, sovereign state for the Tamil people in their homeland which comprised the northern and eastern provinces". For the first time since independence both Sinhala and Tamil peoples were confronted with the prospect of a two-state island where for the past 181 years (since 1815) there had been just one. If ever there was a historic watershed in the affairs of the island this was it. But its significance was not spelt out to the Sinhala people by their leaders who chose to sweep such an uncomfortable nettle under the carpet.

While all this was happening around it, the SLFP government of Mrs. Bandaranaike was in its post-coalition quandary. The expulsion of the Trotskyist and Communist parties from the coalition was part of a late rightward swing under her late husband's nephew, Felix Dias Bandaranaike who was Minister of Finance. He was beginning to eat his earlier words about the "rapacious West" and to woo foreign investment from that very area. The SLFP government under his influence was devoid of a coherent political ideology. It embarked on the 1977 general election lulled into a false sense of security by the nationalised, thoroughly sycophantic press. Seldom has the enormous political cost of controlling the press to the very people who control it been better demonstrated than at the general election of 1977.

In a general election held in a democracy in any part of the world it would be hard to find an equal to the rout of a sitting government as was suffered by Mrs. Bandaranaike in 1977. The SLFP had 91 members in the outgoing Parliament. Of them only two survived — Mrs Bandaranaike herself and her deputy Maithripala Senanayake, the latter by a whisker. Six new SLFP MPs were also elected, making a total of eight in a Parliament of 168 seats. It was just over five per cent of the total number of seats despite getting 29 per cent of the total votes polled. On the other hand the UNP with 51 per cent of the total votes polled secured 140 seats or 83 per cent of the total number of seats — a classic example of the distortion of party representation caused by the "first-past-the-post" system of election. All the left-wing Sinhala parties were routed completely, failing to secure a single seat in Parliament for the first time since independence.

But what of the TULF who were contesting a general election for the very first time and had campaigned openly for a separate state for the Tamil people? In the most significant result of the entire 1977 general election the TULF was swept into Parliament on an ava-lanche of votes — an estimated 69 per cent of the votes polled in the northern and eastern provinces going to them. With 18 seats in the new Parliament it was the second largest party and its leader, Amrithalingam, became leader of the opposition.

The true significance of the enormous electoral victory of the TULF was played down then and continues to be played down to this day. In the last general election held under peaceful conditions, in a free vote without any intimidation, the vast majority of the Tamil people voted in favour of a separate state for themselves. For the Sinhala people and their leaders it was so disquieting a phenom-enon that they have not been able publicly to acknowledge it or to work out its inevitable conclusions. The entire issue has been swept under the carpet; a conspiracy of silence has helped render this a non-event. On the contrary it is widely asserted by all Sinhala leaders, and by repetition sanctified, that it is Pirabhakaran and his "thugs" who want a separate state and not the majority of the Tamil people. Such a travesty of the truth is a grave disservice to the Sinhala people for it leads them into war on a false premise and portrays Pirabhakaran as master of a movement of which he is but the slave.

The true nature of Tamil nationalism came through with crystal clarity in the 1977 general election. The Tamil people revealed themselves as a nation desiring a state of their own. The Sinhala leadership refused to acknowledge or understand, much less ex-plain to their people, the far-reaching significance of this. From that insensitiveness it was but a short step to repression and then to war. The will of an entire people is being thwarted with the ultimate object of crushing that will. What will be the enormous cost in lives and treasure and the eventual futility of that exercise, only time will tell.

The TULF was committed to securing an independent Tamil state if at all possible by negotiation with the government. And the negotiations commenced early. Even if a separate state was contemplated as a distant possibility by the government an agreed outcome might have been possible. But the prospect of a separate state was ruled out at the very outset aborting any chance of a real negotiation. Once again the actions of the Sinhala government confirmed the assertions of the young Tamil militants that an independent state for the Tamils cannot be won by negotiation with the Sinhala government but could only be obtained by recourse to armed struggle. Scepticism about the political process had alienated the young militants from the Federal Party and was soon to alienate them from the TULF as well.

The absolute conviction that their end could be obtained only by war led several of the young militant groups into contacts with Tamil nationalist elements in the adjoining Indian state of Tamilnadu and also with the Indian equivalent of the CIA — the Research and Analysis Wing (RAW) of the Indian Central Government. The latter was casting about to find a counter to the openly pro-USA stance of the newly-elected UNP government which was perceived as a potential threat to Indian interests in the region. They thought the young Tamil militants could be a convenient tool in their hands and acceded to the latter's requests for military training and modern arms. Little did they imagine how intransigent their newfound clients would be. Perhaps they hoped also to appease Tamil nationalism in Tamilnadu and so postpone the evil day of its emergence as a full-fledged national independence movement in India.

The euphoria of its stunning victory in the 1977 general election led the UNP government into giving the Tamil problem a low priority. With five-sixths of the seats in Parliament, it was able to carry out its promised constitutional reform even though the TULF declined to participate in any of the preliminaries and also in the eventual legislation giving effect to it. The Second Republic with an executive president on the French model came into being in 1978. The promised economic policies too were rapidly implemented giving a great boost to economic growth. It stopped short, however, of privatising the host of government corporations, retaining that incubus on the private sector for the political patronage which it afforded.

The UNP Government of President Jayawardene hoped that rapid economic growth from which the Tamil people too would benefit might quench the fires of Tamil nationalism as the Tamil people were renowned for a materialistic bent of mind. It was unable to comprehend the dynamics within the Tamil nation. In the economic sphere the government was forward-looking and aspired to rejoin the world and compete in its markets but politically it was inward and backward-looking. The last thing the UNP Government bargained for was the Tamil groups resorting to the military option.

The events of July 1983 rocked the Government. The first LTTE ambush of a small army patrol in Jaffna marked the beginning of the military conflict. It showed vividly the professionalism of the LTTE in military operations and the quality of their weapons.

It gave an unmistakable foretaste of the formidable nature of the military challenge. The predictable Sinhala response (this time on a thoroughly organised basis) of attacks on Tamil civilians and their property in the Sinhala areas took place on a countrywide scale and with particular ferocity in Colombo. The Government failed to deploy the military immediately in support of the police forces to suppress the rioting, fearing perhaps that the military may join in the attacks on the Tamil population in reprisal for their losses in Jaffna. Whatever the reason, the Government was momentarily shown-up as helpless in the face of violent national uprisings in both north and south.

The attacks on the Tamils in the Sinhala areas were eventually quelled by military means but the episode marked another decisive turning point in the country's affairs. The Government's failure was on three fronts. It failed to deploy the army immediately against the Sinhala gangs killing and burning Tamil civilians and looting and destroying their property. It failed to safeguard Tamil prisoners in the main prison in Colombo leading to two prison riots resulting in the deaths of over 50 Tamil detainees awaiting trial. It failed to bring the perpetrators of these crimes to justice. Inevitably then, the Government forfeited any claims it could make to equal justice under the law for Tamil citizens. Admittedly Tamils still live in the Sinhala areas but they do so with little confidence in either the police or the judicial system. Once again Pirabhakaran's thesis that the

Sinhala government was a government of the Sinhala people for the Sinhala people and from which Tamils could expect no justice was proved to the hilt. The conclusion followed inexorably that the Tamils could expect a secure future only in a state of their own.

The stage was now set for war but nobody on the Sinhala side had the slightest inkling of how severe and protracted a conflict with a nationalist movement could be. The nearly exact parallel of Britain and Eire was not even mentioned. There was a mistaken confidence that the war would be short and quickly ended with the crushing of the Tamil separatists. The minister entrusted with national security (i.e. the conduct of the war) stated there were only 300 "hard core terrorists" implying they could be snuffed out in no time at all. The ignorance of Sinhala politicians of what was going on in what had by now become virtually another country was nothing short of monumental. All wars start with vain hopes of a swift ending and all have dragged on for years. The only exception is the recent Gulf war where these hopes were fulfilled by the overwhelming technical superiority of the US forces — a factor totally absent in Sri Lanka.

7

The Presidential System and the "Rump" Parliament

The Gaullist constitution of France's Fifth Republic ushered in a period of remarkable political stability in that country after the welter of short-lived governments of the post- World War II Fourth Republic. The crumbling of the French empire commencing with the military defeat at Dien Bien Phu in Vietnam, the quagmire of the Algerian war of independence and the debacle of the Suez war had brought France to the very nadir of her fortunes. However, there was a saviour — Charles de Gaulle — waiting in the wings till the time was ripe. His requirement was a fundamental constitutional change to entrench a powerful, directly elected head of state and executive — the executive president. That secured he set about resurrecting the glory of France. The transformation of France that followed, making her one of the power-houses of European modernization and progress, is one of the great success stories of current European history.

The separation of powers and a bi-polar power structure of elected legislature and elected executive had been one of France's contributions at the time of the war of American independence. The constitution of the USA owes far more to Paris than to Westminster. With the Gaullist constitution of the Fifth Republic, France was returning to its own precepts, practising what it had preached. The form of cabinet, however, was different from that in the USA for in France the cabinet is formed from members of the legislature as in Britain. It was a synthesis of a bi-polar power structure with the Westminster system.

The constitution of the Second Republic (1978) in Sri Lanka was modelled on that of France, with but one exception. The electoral system was based on proportional representation whereas France had a modified "first-past-the-post" system with a run-off between the first two candidates where the first had not received at least 50 per cent of the votes polled in the first instance. In one bound Sri Lanka became the only member of the Commonwealth with so un-British and avant garde a constitution. And it all happened without public debate or even awareness of the profundity of the change.

To the questions "How did it happen?" and "Why?" no clear answers have been given yet. The contexts were different; up to 1978 Sri Lanka had not suffered the political instability that had plagued the Fourth Republic. A bi-polar power structure was entirely foreign to Sri Lankan politicians. Proportional representation was, and remains, a mystery compounded by a deep regret at the disappearance of bye-elections and the local constituency MP. One can only hazard a guess as to why the French system was chosen. It would not be too far-fetched to suggest that, perhaps, the principal reason was psychological — the temperament of the man who rode the crest of the wave in 1977 — Junius Richard Jayawardene.

He was a distinctly Gaullist figure. At the age of 36 he became the first Finance Minister of the newly-independent country. From then on he regarded himself as a man of destiny into whose hands power must some day gravitate. Like de Gaulle he had had his ups and downs. All his life he had worked within a Westminster-type of constitutional framework with its in-built checks and balances. He was clear-sighted enough to see the lamentable state to which 30 years of such government had reduced the country. The final seven years under Mrs. Bandaranaike had brought the country to its knees economically. Clearly a radical change was needed — and the rising economic miracle of France, led by a succession of strong presidents after de Gaulle, beckoned irresistibly. There is little doubt that he felt he could emulate their example if he had the same equipment to hand.

The desire for a strong executive had been latent in constitutional thinking among Sri Lankan politicians from the very beginning. The cabinet form of government was thought conducive towards that end. The executive presidency was a further step in that direction.

There was, however, a fundamental difference of great significance, and one which soon became apparent, between the

Westminster type of cabinet government and the executive presidency. In the former the prime minister had the sole power to decide on the dissolution of Parliament but in doing so he himself had to face re-election. That situation changed dramatically under the executive presidency. The president, like the prime minister earlier, could decide on the dissolution of Parliament in his sole discretion but when Parliament was dissolved the president stayed on for the rest of his term. It was a power which Mr Jayawardene was to use with great effect in 1987 to force the Indo-Sri Lanka Peace Accord through a reluctant Parliament. Parliament could be, and without much ado was, browbeaten by the president.

The real test of the system, however, is whether it performed well, or ill, in the governance of the country. In the economic sphere the answer must be an unequivocal affirmative. The liberalisation of the economy by the relaxation of controls was carried out vigorously. A large irrigation-cum-hydro-power scheme in the Sinhala part of the country was completed in double quick time. Foreign investment and modernization of the infrastructure went ahead. The one failure in the economic sphere, and a very costly failure at that, was the sufferance of the continued existence of the government corporations.

In the political sphere, however, the record of the first presidency was much more questionable. And it was in respect of the ethnic problem that the president's weakness was exposed. At the very outset in 1977 he had told the TULF that a separate state for the Tamils, even as a distant possibility, was out of the question. He was then made aware that that decision would undermine the credibility of the TULF and of the democratic political process in general in the eyes of the militant Tamil groups. The president was playing straight into their hands and providing them proof positive that nothing short of war would meet their ends. Of course there was no inkling then, least of all in the president's mind, how serious the conflict would be and how dubious the outcome. Nevertheless, he understood very well the need to grasp this nettle and at least keep the discussion going.

His first effort in this direction was to develop a consensual stand with all the Sinhala political parties and such of the Tamil parties as would participate, in respect of the ethnic problem. But this failed as the SLFP refused to participate and sought instead a declaration of the government's policy perhaps with a view to making political capital of it. Indeed, the government had no policy other than trying to preserve the status quo, i.e. the unitary state which was the colonial entity, Ceylon.

Then came the events of 1983 referred to in the preceding chapter. They demonstrated the inevitability, indeed the actual existence, of a state of war. It was clear that the Tamil militants — the term "terrorists" was now widely used — were well armed and well trained and that the conflict would be a guerilla war fought on their home ground and with the initiative lying largely with them. There was little doubt that both arms and training had been supplied them by India i.e. the Indian Central Government, but diplomatic relations, though strained, were preserved. It was also known that the state of Tamilnadu was backing the militants in a variety of ways short of supplying volunteers for the actual fighting.

The government laid down as a firm and non-negotiable condition the surrender of arms by the militants as an essential prerequisite to any negotiations. There was not the remotest prospect that this requirement would ever be complied with by militant groups who had for years predicted that nothing short of war would secure a separate state for the Tamils. The government's requirement was, therefore, a commitment to war. But the prospects were very forbidding. The army was ill-prepared for a guerilla war; the navy was unable to establish an effective cordon sanitaire in the seas between the two countries to prevent the smuggling into the Tamil areas of arms, ammunition and other war supplies; hard-earned and scarce foreign exchange needed for the development effort was being diverted in ever-increasing amounts to the war effort. The government cast about for a solution and came up with the idea of informal discussions between a non-official Sinhala delegation and the militant groups. The Indian government proffered its good offices and talks were held at the unlikely venue of Thimpu, the capital of the Himalayan kingdom of Bhutan. The Sinhala delegation was led by Harry Jayawardene, a brother of the president and a leading lawyer in Colombo. The LTTE, represented by members of their political wing, and several other Tamil militant groups participated. The proceedings were secret, and still are, but the talks failed to provide any solution. They would, however, have served to enlighten the Sinhala side of the determination of the Tamils to secure a state of their own and their willingness to pay whatever price it would cost them in lives and treasure and hardship for their people.

With the breakdown of the Thimpu talks, the fighting escalated. The government hoped that the Thimpu rhetoric would be just that and no more and that under heavy military pressure the militants would crack and sue for peace. That, however, was not to be. The army's Vadamaradchchi campaign was severely contested and there was a clear prospect of urban guerilla warfare in population centres such as Jaffna with heavy loss of civilian lives. A large efflux of Tamil residents of the northern province to the Indian state of Tamilnadu had already commenced and thus India was dragged into the vortex of the problem. Under heavy pressure from Tamilnadu the Indian Central Government (now under Rajiv Gandhi) intervened by air-dropping relief supplies on population centres in the northern province. This was done against the express wishes and protests of the Sri Lanka government. There was little doubt that further intervention, possibly of a military nature, was in prospect.

In the 39-year history of independent Ceylon (and later Sri Lanka) this was the first time that foreign intervention based on the naked use of force had taken place. The Indian Government was no stranger to such strong arm tactics within its own sphere of influence, having already intervened militarily in Goa and East Pakistan (to establish Bangladesh). It was now on the verge of a similar intervention on behalf of its clients, the Tamil militant groups.

It was at this point that the greatest volte face in modern Sri Lankan history took place. And it was possible only because of the existence of the executive presidency. The president decided to withdraw Sri Lankan forces from the northern and eastern provinces and invite Indian military forces to come in and disarm the Tamil militant groups, to merge temporarily the northern and eastern provinces and to offer to this entity a measure of autonomy on the lines of the Indian federation. Mr Gandhi had always considered the last to be the best answer to Tamil aspirations and was against a separate state for them as that could set off irresistible demands from Tamilnadu for similar independence from the Indian Union. The "Peace Accord", as it was called, was based upon a profound misunderstanding, by both Mr Gandhi and Mr Jayawardene of the intensity and uncompromising nature of Tamil nationalism. Both underestimated its willingness to fight for its cause against all comers if necessary.

The accord was almost universally unpopular with the Sinhala people regardless of their political affiliations. The governing party itself openly opposed it as did the opposition, the Buddhist clergy and the left-wing parties including the militant JVP. The Prime Minister (then Mr Premadasa who later became President) and the Minister of National Security both refused to attend the signing ceremony in Colombo for which Mr Gandhi came down from New Delhi. At an inspection of a guard-of-honour shortly after the signing a naval rating broke ranks and struck Mr Gandhi with the butt-end of his rifle but, mercifully, caused no injury. Rioting and civil unrest broke out all over the Sinhala areas. The Shri Lankan army was flown out of the northern and eastern provinces in the Indian Air Force planes which had brought the Indian troops in. The Sri Lankan troops were landed at airports in the Sinhala areas of the country and were immediately deployed against their rioting compatriots. The uprising was suppressed with considerable loss of life. The President threatened openly to dissolve Parliament if it did not pass the peace accord and its consequential provisions and in the event the threat proved sufficient. The recalcitrant ministers, including the Prime Minister came to heel and backed off from opposing the President's strategy. The necessary legislation was passed. The executive presidency had asserted successfully its supremacy over Parliament and, even more, its ability to adopt and implement policies which were universally unpopular but which it deemed to be in the long-term national interest.

The accord laid the responsibility of disarming the militant Tamil groups on the Indians. While they were successful with most of the groups, the LTTE proved recalcitrant. Pirabhakaran was flown to New Delhi and after considerable arm-twisting there agreed. But shortly after his return, on a dispute with the Indian troops over their handing over to the Sri Lankan authorities of some of his lieutenants (15 of whom committed suicide by swallowing their cyanide capsules) a final rupture took place and the LTTE went to war against the Indian Peace Keeping Force (IPKF). Mr Gandhi had misjudged the extent of his leverage over his client for he had reckoned without the fanatic intensity of Tamil nationalism. Two and a half years of continuous guerilla warfare produced only a stalemate and in the long-run Mr Gandhi paid with his own life to what by then had become the deadliest of his many enemies.

The Sri Lankan side of the accord had two elements. One was the reversal of the main items of discriminatory legislation of the early years of independence. "Sinhala only", the sacred cow of all Sinhala political parties, was abandoned at a stroke and Tamil and English became official languages on the same footing as Sinhala. The language issue disappeared from the political agenda apparently for good. No Sinhala political party so much as breathes a word about it now. So also went the statelessness and votelessness of the Tamil plantation-worker population. It was now clear to all and sundry that not the democratic parliamentary process but war had brought about these salutary changes. The assertion of the Tamil militants that only by force of arms could they secure justice for themselves had been amply vindicated. Thereafter, to invite them to return to the democratic process which had brought them nothing and abandon war which had yielded so much, must seem farcical in the extreme to them.

The second element was a high degree of local autonomy for the merged north-east province. In order to mask the appearance of special treatment for that area, a whole system of provincial councils, one for each province of the country, was devised and passed by Parliament. It was rejected by the LTTE out of hand as bearing no resemblance to the independent sovereign state for which they were fighting. The IPKF then put up their own puppet regime to run the north-east provincial council but that too, despite a unilateral declaration of independence by it, was short-lived as events were soon to prove.

Both Mr Gandhi and Mr Jayawardene thought that devolution of powers to an administrative unit in the north-east, on lines similar to the federal arrangements between the Centre and the states in India, would lay the Tamil problem to rest once and for all. So the provincial council legislation was very much influenced by the Indian Constitution. Neither, however, took account of what by then had become *the* most important factor in the situation which was that the LTTE was now heavily armed, battle-hardened in fighting a guerilla war against a professional army and was led brilliantly and fanatically by leaders with an *idee fixe* — that they would fight on till they had won a separate sovereign state for the Tamil people. The situation in fact was a post-federal one for even a formal federal arrangement is impossible when the federating units already have armies of their own not subject to any joint command. To offer an administrative devolution of powers to a provincial council to meet a problem which was post-federal in nature shows the degree of misunderstanding of the realities of the situation.

The extent of the retreat from reality is even better illustrated by an earlier event. Shortly after the 1983 upheaval, Parliament passed the sixth amendment to the constitution which declared it illegal to advocate publicly the establishment of a separate state in the island and requiring all public officers and members of Parliament to take an oath affirming their loyalty to the existing unitary (in the geographical sense) state. The object was to legislate unity and by so doing halt or reverse the break-up of the state which was so manifestly gathering momentum. The immediate effect, however, was the very opposite of that intended. All the TULF MPs quit Parliament never to return. As they had been elected on the first-past-the-post system of election, bye-elections had to be held to replace them. But the military situation in the Tamil areas made this impossible.

Thus at one stroke Parliament converted itself into a "rump" representative only of the Sinhala areas. The constitution did not provide for any such eventuality, so very real doubts can be entertained as to the constitutionality of Parliament thereafter and as to the validity of laws passed by it. Whatever the legal niceties of the situation may be, it had certainly lost its moral authority to pass laws applicable in the Tamil areas or to raise taxes from those areas which were now unrepresented in it.

In fact from 1987 the writ of the government had ceased to run in the Tamil areas which were de facto under military rule by day (in areas where the military was present) and under the rule of the militant groups, latterly the LTTE alone, by night. The civil administration existed on sufferance from the militant groups and its main live link with Colombo was to draw salaries from that source. Indeed this was the one activity on which all parties to the conflict were enthusiastically agreed!

The sixth amendment is, perhaps, the best illustration of the depths of confusion prevailing in the minds of executive and legislature alike about the nature of society and of the state which serves it. The elementary fact is that the glue which binds a society together and supports the state is the freely given consent of the governed. Consent by its very nature is voluntary and cannot be secured by coercion or legislation. Such efforts may produce a temporary acquiescence but not the permanent bond of freely given consent. The colonial state of Ceylon was not held together by consent. It was held together by the force of imperial arms. If such a state was to survive as a single entity it could do so only on the basis of the freely given consent of all parties living in it. Unity cannot be legislated still less imposed by force. The very concepts of consent and force are mutually exclusive.

When the Tamil people voted overwhelmingly in 1977 for a separate state of their own it signalled the end of the unitary state and the consequential prospect of a two-state island. Can a unitary state be resurrected by force? Can the Tamil people's express wish for a state of their own be suppressed by force of arms? On the level of practical possibility the answers to these questions must be in the negative on the basis of historical experience and current knowledge. But by far the more disturbing aspect of these questions is what moral justification the Sinhala people and their leaders have for denying to the Tamil people a state of their own. These are issues that need to be addressed in the open and become the subject of serious public discussion. To sweep them under the carpet is to invite a state of continuous war and destruction and the systematic pauperization of both nations.

8

War and Presidential Control of the Military

The relationship of civil government to the military machine which has the monopoly of force in the state is fraught with difficulty even in the mature democracies. In the USA the friction between the President on the one hand and the military-industrial complex on the other, goes back to President Eisenhower's days and still lurks not far below the surface. Political decisions regarding arms reduction are invariably consensual ones taken after carefully prepared consultations with the military. In Mr Gorbachev's first overthrow hard-line elements of the military played an important part. Conversely, the collapse of that coup was due to Mr Yeltsin being successful in converting a large part of the military to strictly constitutional conduct. In peace time, the interplay between civil and military powers though not publicly visible is one of the most sensitive and uncertain areas in modern states. In times of war, however, the relationship is eased by the existence of a common enemy but even so political strategy and military necessity do not always correspond.

The difficulty of the relationship is illustrated by the experience of many of the new states that emerged from de-colonization. Pakistan has had a succession of military coups and long periods of military government. So has Bangladesh and Ghana and Nigeria. Indonesia has been under military rule under the guise of "guided democracy" for the last 27 years. India has not suffered this fate but after several wars with Pakistan and a traumatic Himalayan conflict with China has had to maintain one of the world's largest standing armies. This has caused great problems for civil government. Supplies for the military have influenced foreign policy (e.g. the special relationship with the former Soviet Union and the current edging towards the USA) as well as domestic politics (the Bofors case which seriously affected Rajiv Gandhi's political fortunes). The use of the military in support of foreign policy has entailed a price, especially where covert operations are concerned, to the extent of compromising the civil government and pre-empting its decisions.

Sri Lanka has had no military conflicts with external powers but the high level of domestic unrest has brought the military very much to the forefront. The first test was the 1971 JVP insurrection which demonstrated the unpreparedness of both civil and military authorities for such a challenge despite reasonably competent intelligence services. To cope with the initial shock the government had to obtain military support mainly from India. The uprising (by young rural radicals discontented with the high levels of unemployment and alienated by a middle-class dominated Westminster-style of parliamentary government in which it was virtually impossible for them to participate) was bloodily crushed with heavy loss of life almost entirely on the side of the insurgents and with relatively few military casualties. The ring-leaders were arrested, tried publicly, convicted and sentenced to long terms of imprisonment. Though the military was given a free hand, the supremacy of the civil government was maintained. In fact the Government made a systematic attempt at rehabilitating the lower rank of the insurgents who had been apprehended during the struggle. Mrs Bandaranaike's government emerged creditably from this first test.

The first hiccup in civil-military relations came in 1983, five years after the inauguration of presidential rule. In July of that year came the first organised LTTE ambush of an army patrol in the north. The patrol was virtually wiped out and the young officer in command killed. The bodies were brought to Colombo for burial and that sparked off the largest ever (and so far the last) pogrom on Tamil civilians in Colombo and other Sinhala areas. The situation clearly warranted military intervention for the restoration of law and order but the President vacillated for several days. There can be little doubt that the reason for this was his uncertainty as to how the military would react. There was ample evidence that the pogrom, at least initially, was a carefully pre-planned thing and it is possible that supporters of, and sympathisers with, the Sinhala army who were part of the political hierarchy were behind it. Whatever that may be, the civil-military relationship was put to an unprecedently severe test and the President wobbled very badly. In due course the army was called in and did suppress the disturbances but only after a heavy loss of life among the Tamil population living in the Sinhala areas and incalculable damage to their homes and property. And for the first time since independence there was open discord and recrimination between the civil authority and the military.

Hard on the heels of this followed open warfare in the northern and eastern provinces and the progressive collapse of the civil authority there. It is interesting that from the outset the term used to describe the conflict was "war" and not "civil war". There was a general understanding, even though not openly expressed, that the conflict was with a separate state albeit a purported one. Armed Tamil groups began guerilla warfare all over the northern and eastern provinces — an area the size of Belgium — in rough ill-roaded terrain. Their object was to drive the Sri Lankan army out of what they regarded as, and openly asserted to be, the Tamil homeland. Even at this late stage the government could not discern the nature of Tamil nationalism and entered the conflict regarding it as a drive to flush out a few "terrorist" groups. The failure of the civil government to comprehend what was and is essentially a political issue brought the military into a conflict for which they were ill-prepared and of which the eventual outcome was, at best, dubious.

The government then embarked on attempts to secure assistance for the military from the western powers. The effort was unsuccessful due to the diplomatic failure to convince world opinion of the practicality of enforcing unity by military means. There were world-wide misgivings about the efficacy of such a policy — let alone its moral justification. By this time the publicity campaigns of the international Eelam lobby were well orchestrated doubtless with covert Indian diplomatic support.

Then came the Vadamaradchchi campaign — a major military effort in the northern province aimed at capturing Jaffna eventually. It was a case of civil government well aware of the international risks of such an effort caving in to a gung-ho military establishment. The army met with stiff resistance from the outset and the extent of Indian military support for the Tamil groups soon became evident. As a warning shot across the bows of the Sri Lankan government the Indian Air Force dropped relief supplies on civilian centres in the area of the fighting ostensibly for civilian relief. Though never openly threatened it was clear that India would not tolerate the overwhelming of the Tamil militant groups which it had armed. The President was left in no doubt of the likelihood of armed Indian intervention — dressed up as a humanitarian mission to safeguard the civilian population on their behalf. The military had got the civil government into the worst international imbroglio since independence.

The events that followed, described in detail in the preceding chapter, constituted an attempt by the civil authority to wrest the initiative from the military. The withdrawal of the army from the north and east to tackle the growing civil war in the Sinhala areas, particularly in the southern province, was extremely unpopular. For a brief period Indian naval forces stood outside the port of Colombo to prop up the President. If the President did a volte face in inviting the Indian forces, the Indian Central Government did an equally stunning volte face in switching its support from the Tamil militant groups to the Sri Lankan government. No doubt both sides hoped that such dramatic reversals of policy would yield quick solutions to all the problems. They assumed that the disarming of the Tamil militants, which was the essential prerequisite for their preferred solutions (for Mr Gandhi a federal constitution on Indian lines; for Mr Jayawardene some arrangement less overtly federal) could be quickly accomplished. It was the illusory nature of that assumption on which the whole peace accord eventually foundered. The initiative of the civil authority proved as ineffectual as that of the military.

In the meantime the Sinhala areas of the country slipped into turmoil and civil war with the second JVP insurrection. From 1987 to 1989 there raged a ferocious conflict which cost an estimated 40,000 lives. Slaughter on such a scale and of such savagery was unprecedented in the country's history. It was a blood-letting many times greater than that of the war in the north-east. The rule of law was deliberately relaxed and the military was given the right to bury or cremate their victims without a coroner's inquest. Even the few restraints that continued to apply to the military were unknown to the numerous "hit-squads" spawned on both sides. The relatives of victims banded together for vengeance. Modern weaponry was in unauthorised hands and was used to deadly effect. When the JVP leaders were caught by the military they were summarily executed with little or no reference to the president and not a hint of due process of law.

By then a new president (Premadasa) had taken office and a fresh attempt was made to wrest the initiative for the civil authority. The former president's policy in regard to the disarming of the LTTE and refusal to negotiate with them until they were disarmed was reversed. The new president was realist enough to declare that it was impossible to disarm the LTTE. The Indian Army's failure to achieve that end after two and half years of fighting was proof of that. He decided on talks with the LTTE without any pre-conditions and the talks took place in Colombo over a long period of 14 months. Even the possibility of absorbing the guerilla forces of the LTTE and other groups into the Sri Lankan army so as to preserve the unity of the country (a country can have only one army not two rival ones) was on the cards. The LTTE was assisted by the government in its conflict with other Tamil groups, notably the puppet organisation of the Indian Army known as the Tamil National Army. These measures, especially the arming of the LTTE, were unpopular with the Sri Lankan army and behind the President's back a military build-up took place in the eastern province to counter the growing power and influence of the LTTE there. This roused the LTTE's suspicions and led to their pre-emptive strike in June 1990 on police and military establishments in the eastern province which resulted in the break-up of the negotiations. The President's initiative lay in dust and ashes around his feet and a gung-ho military was once more calling the shots both figuratively and literally. By then the Indian forces had withdrawn and everybody was back to square one.

Both sides were now better armed, trained and led with a resulting sophistication in tactics and strategy. The Sri Lankan forces are beginning to use, and depend increasingly on, air power. Demands for such equipment are increasing. The lessons of the Vietnam war where massive air power was used against guerillas without decisive effect do not seem to have been learned. The temptation to use air bombardment to soften up a target before ground attack is very great. But the use of air power has also political implications. It is tantamount to admitting that the war is being waged against a foreign country. Not even at the height of the JVP insurgency were air strikes used against them in the Sinhala areas. The use of air power is a clear instance of the prevailing of military over civilian judgements.

The military judgement of the situation is, apparently, the simplistic notion that Tamil separatist groups were miscreants who had to be put down as quickly and as thoroughly as possible. The true nature of the Tamil uprising — that it is a nationalist upsurge, strong enough to inspire people to enormous sacrifices, including the sacrifice of their lives for their cause — was not understood. The facts that a large diaspora of Tamils of all classes had taken place, that a great many of them were well-placed to influence international opinion and secure international support, that they could mobilize considerable resources in foreign exchange for their cause, that they had the capacity to supply arms to their compatriots on their home-ground, were given little weightage in military thinking.

The LTTE's forces had, single-handed, taken on and held the IPKF at bay through two and half years of sustained guerilla warfare. But even this has not moderated the over-confident mentality of the Sinhala military leadership. Pronouncements are made regularly about the "final campaign", "the conclusion of the war by year-end", that "victory is in sight" etc. It is like an old movie, a re-run of the US military's predictions during the 10 years of the Vietnam war. The President on the other hand is torn between a deeper understanding of the problem, especially after 14 months of secret talks with the most articulate and thoughtful members of the LTTE's political wing, and the somewhat naive and misplaced enthusiasm of the military.

In the meantime the financial implications of the war for the economy continue to be serious. So far the demands of the military even for the expensive air war equipment have been met. As higher and higher levels of military technology are employed by the Sri Lankan forces the foreign exchange costs, already high, are bound to escalate in geometrical progression. Every military push on the ground raises the military's demands for funds. Eventually this must lead to the progressive curtailment of the civil government's social programmes and policies. Already infrastructure maintenance, even at the low pre-war levels, is beginning to show the strain. The government is propped up only by foreign aid. Any decline in that support or any dramatic increase in military demands for funds could imperil the very existence of civil government and even lead to its overthrow by the military in the interests of mobilizing all of the country's resources for the war effort.

The relationship that obtained between President Premadasa and the military can be inferred by reading between the lines of public pronouncements and by being sensitive to the nuances. The President, like his predecessor, had held the defence portfolio throughout. But it was the junior Minister of Defence who had direct dealings with the military. The first junior minister under Premadasa was Ranjan Wijeratne. He had a very close rapport with the military and was a strong advocate of their views and demands in the inner councils of government. At times he, rather than the President, appeared to be the living embodiment of the Sinhala cause. In one of his more rambunctious moments in Parliament he portrayed the conflict in very personal terms, saying it had to be either Pirabhakaran or himself — there was no mention at all of the President. Wijeratne asserted regularly in Parliament that Pirabhakaran was already dead — he constantly used the sobriquet "the late Pirabhakaran" — but that did not prevent him issuing open challenges to Pirabhakaran for single-handed combat to settle the issue between the races one way or the other. He was the perfect embodiment of the aggressive military attitude and there is good reason to believe that he covertly acquiesced in the sabotage of the President's talks with the LTTE. The possibility of Tamil militant groups being absorbed into the country's military forces and the supply of arms by the goverment to the LTTE to help them in their fight against the puppet organisation of the IPKF at the President's instance were all factors that contributed to the unease in the relationship between the President and the military.

With Wijeratne's assassination (blown up by a car bomb located either in his own car or in a van parked by the roadside and detonated by a suicide bomber as Wijeratne's car drew abreast) the situation changed. He was replaced as junior minister of defence by a presidential loyalist — none other than the Prime Minister himself, D.B. Wijetunge. The very fact that the Prime Minister should hold concurrently a junior portfolio shows both the level to which the prime ministership has fallen and the President's need for a person in that post whose loyalty to the President is greater than to the cause of the military. The appointment is clear evidence of the President's need to regain control over the military.

As the fortunes of war waxed and waned for each side, the waters were muddied by a move to impeach the President. It was made formally by the opposition in Parliament but was inspired by a breakaway faction of the governing party which was dissatisfied with the "one-show" style of the President and which suspected him also of treasonable conduct in his dealings with the LTTE during the aborted negotiations. The move turned out to be a damp squib but showed that with the rising tempo of the war anything done or said either overtly or covertly against the military would be used to raise the accusation of unpatriotism. On the other hand the President's subservience to the military line could well lead to the degradation of his position and even to an eventual overthrow.

When de Gaulle came to power in France founding the Fifth Republic, he faced very much the same situation in respect of the war of Algerian independence. But he succeeded in overcoming military opposition by the sheer force of his personality and his glowing record of patriotism in leading the Free French fighting forces in the second World War. And he carried the people along with him as well in recognising Algerian independence.

Is there such a patriot in the wings in Sri Lanka who can lead the Sinhala people towards a clear-eyed recognition of the realities of their situation and towards the changes necessary to achieve peace even against an obdurate military machine by now accustomed to the spoils of war?

9

The Failure to Re-assert Presidential Supremacy

The progressive decline in presidential supremacy in the power balance within the state is best illustrated by a comparison between the two presidencies — those of Jayawardene and Premadasa. The preceding chapter showed that even in Jayawardene's time there had been two difficult patches (1983 and 1987). He did, however, retain the initiative for reasons which will be discussed presently.

A comparison between two men of such widely differing background, personality and temperament and of two very unequal periods of rule must necessarily be an invidious one. Nevertheless, a comparison is essential to understand the decline of presidential supremacy and the failure in, or the impossibility of, reasserting it.

The comparison that follows has to do with four key areas, namely, the relationship of each president to Parliament; their own party — the UNP; the military, and India.

Jayawardene had a Parliament totally dominated by his party which had five-sixths of its total membership. Not surprisingly he contrived to extend the life of that Parliament to eleven and a half years to correspond to his whole term. When this Parliament was reduced to a rump by the withdrawal of the TULF MPs his control over it was even greater. When he made his celebrated volte-face in 1987 the whole Parliament, including all but a handful of his own party, opposed him but were browbeaten and figuratively cudgelled into line. In the last years of his Presidency his dominance of Parliament was total

Premadasa did not have the advantage of a compliant Parliament. His party had a little over half its membership and faced a powerful and vocal opposition led by Mrs Bandaranaike supported by a galaxy of legal and histrionic talent. His choice of Prime

Minister of a person of less than mediocre capability in the cut and thrust of parliamentary debate served his government ill and led to defections within his own party.

The decline of presidential influence in Parliament is nothing short of precipitous. To judge by the way the President was heckled by the opposition at the September 1991 opening of Parliament (after its sudden prorogation) it seems unlikely that a recovery in presidential influence can be achieved.

As regards the relationship to the party, Jayawardene was virtually the sole architect of his party — the UNP — having built it up after the 1956 general election debacle. His command of the party's parliamentary group was unquestioned and was clinched by his securing, and holding in his possession, undated letters of resignation from every member of his party. The object of this bizarre arrangement was not to prevent defection to the opposition — that was impossible under the constitution of the second republic which decreed that an MP who defected to another party ipso facto forfeited his seat in Parliament — but to secure an iron discipline within the party. The other side of the coin of Jayawardene's dominance was the abject servility of the UNP MPs of that time, every one of whom complied with the President's requirement.

Premadasa, on the other hand, was much more a primus inter pares and very much on the wrong end of the intellectual balance with several of his eminent colleagues. His preference for the support of mediocrities within the party led to factionalism and finally schism leading to open defiance. This resulted in the expulsion from the party of some of its senior members. All this dissension fuelled an attempt (unsuccessful) by the opposition in Parliament to impeach the President and this was supported by the dissident members of the UNP. His grip over his party was far from secure. Once the rot set in, it was difficult to arrest and still more difficult to reverse. This is just what happened in the case of Premadasa. The electorate itself was roused by highly emotive issues such as the alleged supply of arms to the LTTE on the President's orders. The unease felt at the grassroots seeped up like rising damp to other levels as well.

The chequered course of the relationship between the civil and military elements of the body politic has been set out in the preceding chapter. Jayawardene did things which were highly unpopular with the military and was even briefly, propped up by a show of

Indian military muscle. Premadasa's flirtation with the LTTE was a similar cause for military misgiving (and the relationship could be soured even more seriously if the alleged supply of arms, even an anti-aircraft gun, to the LTTE were proved). As stated in the preceding chapter it is the military rather than the President which is emerging as the champion of the national aspirations of the Sinhala people. If the cause of peace is to be served it is very necessary that the President should succeed eventually in reversing that damaging perception.

It is in the relationship with India that the sharpest divergence between the two presidents has taken place. Jayawardene's rapprochement with Rajiv Gandhi and the Peace Accord which followed was summarily reversed by Premadasa on his assumption of office. There were many reasons for this. Prime Minister Premadasa had been uncompromising in his assertion that India had trained and armed the Tamil militants and he was forthright in his denunciation of such hostile acts. He had had a celebrated confrontation with Rajiv Gandhi in New York and there was little love lost between the two men. He had opposed the Peace Accord which had been concluded by Jayawardene without his knowledge. It had added fuel to the fire of the JVP uprising which it fell to the lot of Premadasa to handle.

All these considerations blinded him to the fact that the Indian army was fighting the LTTE with a view to disarming the latter. If the unitary state in the geographical sense was to be saved there had to be only one army on the island, not two or more. The Indian army was fighting towards this end in trying to disarm the LTTE. The latter was hard pressed by the Indian forces and wanted them out at any cost and this was the common bond that brought them to the negotiation with Premadasa. The President too had much to gain from the withdrawal of the Indian forces; he could satisfy the Sinhala nationalist lobby which was against foreign intervention however necessary; he could cut the ground from underneath the feet of the JVP; he could secure the goodwill of the LTTE and thus hope for a settlement with them which preserved the unity of the country. And he had a fallback position if he failed in the last objective — the Sri Lankan army might do better than the Indians against the LTTE for it would have a stronger motivation as it was fighting to preserve its own country. It was a high-risk strategy which events were soon to prove to have been based on many misjudgements. The JVP fought on even after the Indians left; the LTTE proved unwavering in their commitment to a separate, sovereign state for the Tamil people and the ability of the Sri Lankan army (which has after 18 months of fighting not even attempted to take Jaffna which the Indians did quite early in their campaign) to improve on the Indians' performance is very much open to doubt. The President's request to the Indians to withdraw (or "de-induct" in the quaint Ind-glish in which the diplomatic exchanges were conducted) was responded to not with alacrity but with much foot-dragging despite the widespread unpopularity of the war in India, the heavy casualties they suffered and their signal lack of success against the Tamil guerillas.

With their withdrawal the reversal of Jayawardene's Indian policy was complete and the two countries embarked on an uneasy stand off. Things have not improved even after the fall of Rajiv Gandhi and his replacement first by V.P. Singh and later by Chandra Shekhar and currently by Narasimha Rao who had been Foreign Minister when the Peace Accord was cobbled together. The Indian relationship gave Jayawardene something to fall back on, a solid ally from whom he could draw support for his initiative. He had broken the link between the Indian Central Government and the Tamil militants. Premadasa had sacrificed these advantages and was in an isolated and exposed condition, compounding his many and growing difficulties.

As with Jayawardene so with Premadasa, it is their twists and turns on the ethnic problem that has bedevilled their presidencies. Premadasa's response to the ethnic problem evolved uncertainly through several phases. First came the reversal of Jayawardene's Indian policy, the flirtation with the LTTE and a successful diplomatic campaign (greatly helped by the fall of Rajiv Gandhi in the Indian general election of 1989) to secure the total withdrawal of Indian troops from the island. This was a confident beginning, facing up to the realities of the situation and exercising a political initiative, even though it was a high-risk one, towards a rational solution.

Then came the military backlash covertly subverting the President's initiative by the military build-up in the eastern province behind the President's back. The pre-emptive strike by the LTTE in June 1990 ended the first phase and with it the last real hope of salvaging a single state with a single army. The President's high-risk strategy had gone up in smoke and the Indians were no longer around to pull his chestnuts out of the fire for him.

The second phase was the reversion to the pre-July 1987 policies of the first President i.e. war with the LTTE and a refusal to negotiate with them until they surrendered their arms. He was reverting to a policy which had been tried and had failed, because he had nowhere else to go. The military had now wrested the initiative and he was giving ear to the siren song of military claims regarding the certainty of victory in the war.

The third phase was influenced by battlefield reversals at Mankulam, the Jaffna Fort etc. which gave rise to concern that the military assessments of certain victory were not realistic and that the war could drag on for an unforeseeable length of time. Overtures to the LTTE for negotiations were commenced subject to their accepting certain preconditions such as the surrender of their arms and the personal participation of Pirabhakaran in the negotiations. When the LTTE proved unyielding the surrender of arms was transmuted into a forswearing of the use of force and the Pirabhakaran condition was dropped. When this too did not work the alternative of Thondaman, a senior minister of the government and leader of the plantation Tamil population going to Jaffna for discussions without any preconditions was considered. Thondaman then published what he considered to be a reasonable framework of proposals for discussion with the LTTE recognising that the situation had reached a post-federal stage with the LTTE holding considerable areas of territory in the north-east from which the Sri Lankan army was not strong enough to oust them. They were greeted with a storm of opposition from a wide spectrum of Sinhala nationalist organisations and in fact they stimulated the emergence of new ones. The President did not identify himself too closely with these proposals nor did he repudiate them altogether, indicating the state of uncertainty prevailing on the ethnic problem.

Shortly prior to the Thondaman proposals a parliamentary select committee under the chairmanship of an opposition MP, Mr Mangala Moonesinghe, a member of the SLFP, had been appointed to work out an agreed all-party solution to the ethnic problem. It was hoped that if such agreement was possible it could be the basis of negotiations with the LTTE and other Tamil groups who could contribute to a workable and lasting solution. This was somewhat similar to the all-party conference during the first presidency but was an improvement on that because this time round the SLFP was a participant and one of their members was in fact the chairman of the committee. The first item of the committee's terms of reference is the preservation of the territorial integrity of the state which at one stroke rules out the Tamil demand for a separate state for themselves. Consequently, the only hope of the committee's work bearing any fruit is dependent on the LTTE being militarily reduced to the point at which it is virtually compelled to abandon the main object of its struggle and settle for a lesser goal. Military pressure is therefore the essential element of the present strategy. This is the situation at the time of this writing.

Since the commencement in June 1990 of the current phase of the war there has been a rapid increase in military numbers and influence. At present the ratio of the Sri Lankan armed forces to guerillas is estimated to be 10 to 1 and this is considered sufficient in some circles. In Northern Ireland where a guerilla war has lasted now for nearly 24 years the ratio of British troops and paramilitary forces to guerillas is 100 to 1 and even that high figure has proved inadequate. The terrain in the north-east province of Sri Lanka is much better suited to guerilla operations than in the six counties and two county boroughs of Northern Ireland. These realities are beginning to feed through into military thinking in Sri Lanka. There are already murmurs from military quarters as to the need for total mobilization of the manpower and financial resources of the Sinhala nation if victory is to be won. The Tamil nation is seen to be mobilized in this way and that accounts for their resilience and capacity to keep the fight going interminably. They are not saddled with the expenses of a civil government nor the albatross of a horde of loss-making state corporations. If they are to be beaten they must be taken on an equal footing. The Sinhala people cannot expect victory without heavy sacrifices of an order undreamt of up to now. So goes the military argument and it is not devoid of persuasive logic. Conscription and total mobilization will involve a switch of financial resources from civil to military of such a magnitude as to be impossible under the present constitutional framework as it will entail the suspension of all the social amelioration and development programmes of the civil government. As the intensity of the war escalates, as military technologies of an ever higher level are employed at enormous costs in foreign exchange and as the military establishment itself balloons an early victim could well be civil government itself leaving the military completely dominant.

The stalemate that now exists reveals the President's inability to comprehend the realities of the situation. No doubt this is due partly to the up-beat military assessments he receives and his inability to analyse them realistically. At all levels of government and in the state-controlled media there is an inability or unwillingness or both to understand the true nature of the war i.e. that it is a war waged by the Sinhala government and armed forces to defeat a national uprising of the Tamil nation determined to establish a separate state for themselves in the area in which they live. So a victory in a single engagement is mistaken for a sign of impending victory in the war. And the war goes on with intermittent bursts of activity in different parts of the large area comprising the combined north-east province. The forces of the LTTE have not been vanquished and all overtures to them on the assumption that they are a defeated enemy are doomed to failure from the outset. Negotiations on the basis of equality and reciprocity are the only ones that stand any chance of taking place and bearing any fruit. Any condition such as the forswearing of the use of force will have to be subscribed to by both sides. That is why the surrender of weapons is not a realistic demand for neither side will agree to it and to expect only one side to do so is unilateral and not reciprocal.

All of which goes to show that two states, each equipped with well-organized military forces which are locked in battle with each other, exist. That is the inescapable reality of the situation. And the sooner there is a clear-eyed perception of it the better will be the prospects of peace for both peoples.

10

The Geo-politics of Military Dominance

In this chapter the "military dominance" that will be discussed is not battle-field superiority of the Sri Lankan army over the LTTE but the prevailing of military influence over civil on the ethnic question within the Sri Lankan government in Colombo. The fluctuations in this relationship have been described and discussed in earlier chapters but only from the domestic point of view. It is time now to turn to their international, especially South Asian, implications.

First, and most important, is the effect on India of the ethnic conflict in Sri Lanka and its progressive escalation into guerilla warfare. India is not a homogeneous or monolithic political entity. It is a federal union with a constantly changing balance of power between the centre and the constituent states. It is necessary, therefore, to deal separately with the relationship of the Indian central government and of the state of Tamilnadu to the ethnic problem in Sri Lanka. Indeed at times there have been sharp divergences of interest between the two Indian entities.

The policy of the Indian central government towards the ethnic problem in Sri Lanka has been consistent in two important respects.

The first is the consistently held view that the indigenous Tamils of Sri Lanka had been systematically discriminated against by successive governments in Sri Lanka and redress could be secured for them only by a measure of self-government comparable to that enjoyed by the states in the Indian federal union. In India the latent fissiparous tendencies of the many and diverse ethnic groups settled in linguistic states had been contained by the federal ar-rangements, imperfect though these were. It was a federal form in which the balance of power was tilted strongly in favour of the centre. It had served India well so far and there seemed to be no reason why a similar arrangement in Sri Lanka should not have a similar beneficial effect. The government of the state of Tamilnadu shared this view and urged the Indian central government to lean on the Sri Lankan government to secure such a solution.

Secondly, the Indian central government has consistently supported, and still supports, the territorial integrity of Sri Lanka as a single state encompassing the whole island. And this despite the fact that the single state was in reality a British colonial contraption and that the Indian experience at the point of de-colonization was the opposite, namely, that the colonial entity, the British Raj, was split into two separate, sovereign, independent states — India and Pakistan. The Indian central government's insistence on the territorial integrity of Sri Lanka was not entirely altruistic; rather was it motivated by self-interest in that it would avert demands for total independence by any of the states of the Indian federal union which could lead to the eventual break-up of India. From very early times there had been a strong Dravidian nationalist undercurrent in the southern states and, especially in Tamilnadu, it was not far below the surface. The preservation of Tamil culture from Sanskritic inroads from the north had been the burden of the writings of Periyar E.V. Ramaswamy Naicker. They had inspired the formation of the Dravida Munnetra Kazagham (DMK) and its later variant the All-India Anna DMK which today is one of the strongest regional political parties in India. If the Indian central government supported the establishment of an independent Tamil state in Sri Lanka it would virtually open the flood-gates of Tamil nationalism in India with incalculable consequences for the country as a whole. So the Indian central government resolutely set its face against the establishment of the state of Eelam by the indigenous Tamils of Sri Lanka.

And it was not above making a virtue of necessity in its dealings with the Sri Lankan governments. As a trade-off for upholding the territorial integrity of Sri Lanka the Indian central government did its best to pressurize the Sri Lankan government towards constitutional change to give the indigenous Tamils of the northern and eastern provinces a large measure of self-government similar, covertly if not overtly, to the federal arrangement in India. Mrs Indira Gandhi, during her long tenure of office as prime minister of India, did her best towards this end but was defeated by the stonewalling intransigence of successive Sri Lankan governments. The young Tamil militants had predicted that nothing would come of these efforts by India and the passage of time proved them right.

There then occurred the fateful switch in Indian central government policy and one shrouded in the tightest secrecy as such a high-risk decision had necessarily to be. The Indian central government decided covertly to train and arm the various Tamil militant groups to prepare them for guerilla warfare in the hope that this would make the Sri Lankan government see reason and become more amenable to India's preferred solution — a quasi-federal settlement. It took this step on two very flawed assumptions — first, that such a settlement would satisfy the Tamil militants and second, that having trained and armed the militant groups it could retain influence and control over them. Both these assumptions illustrated the fundamental misconception under which the Indian central government laboured as to the true nature and intensity of nationalism among the indigenous Tamils of the island. It hoped to use Tamil nationalism in Sri Lanka to bolster the Indian union and postpone the evil day when southern Dravidian separatism would rear its ugly head. The Tamil militants, however, were not about to let themselves be used in other people's, even their benefactor's game — they had an agenda of their own from which the geo-political interests of their neighbours and patrons could not deflect them.

And worst of all the Indian central government's decision to arm the militants ended decisively any prospect of a quasi-federal solution which India hankers after, now forlornly, to this day. The means by which it set out to achieve its first objective were self-defeating and will in the long run end in the failure of its second objective as well.

The relationship of the Tamilnadu state government to the ethnic problem in Sri Lanka was different to that of the Indian central government. The ethnic and cultural kinship between the population of Tamilnadu (now around 60 million) and the Tamils of the northern and eastern provinces of Sri Lanka lent a very personal and emotional element to the problem. The valiant and unwavering stand of the indigenous Tamils of the island struck a responsive chord among the Tamil population in the length and breadth of Tamilnadu. Inflammatory talk of genocide by the Sri Lankan forces raised passions and once guerilla warfare started in earnest the large refugee influx into Tamilnadu — only 22 miles across the Palk

Strait from Jaffna — strengthened the ethnic bonds and a state-wide resistance movement was set off. The situation sent shock waves through the entire political spectrum in Tamilnadu and the state government was quick to respond. Camps were established to accommodate the refugees — at this writing there are around 230 camps each housing about 1000 souls — and the Tamil militant groups on the island were permitted to move their organisations to Tamilnadu. Medical treatment was provided for the wounded and financial assistance was given both to the refugees and to the militant organisations. The latter set up a state-wide network of cells for securing moral, material and political support for their struggle. The then chief minister, M.G. Ramachandran, made a much-publicized grant of funds to the LTTE which had emerged early in the day as the largest, best-organised and most uncompromising of the many militant groups. Local private organisations gave covert support in smuggling arms and war supplies across the narrow strait and the banking system in the state was used for the funneling of funds raised internationally by the far-flung Tamil diaspora for the struggle.

When the Jayawardene government and its first Minister of National Security, Athulathmudali, strove to secure a military victory in the Vadamaradchchi campaign the state government's pressure on the Indian central government was such that overt Indian military intervention became imminent. It was averted only by the volte-face of the Gandhi-Jayawardene Peace Accord of July 1987 described earlier.

Rajiv Gandhi's volte-face lay in his switching of Indian central government support from the Tamil militant groups to the Sri Lankan government but he was consistent in trying to secure the Indian central government's first objective of policy i.e. a quasi-federal solution to the ethnic problem in Sri Lanka. The Peace Accord contained express provision towards this end and knowing it could not be achieved so long as the Tamil militants were armed he decided to use Indian forces to disarm them when all efforts at persuasion (finally attempted by him personally in New Delhi in a confrontation with Pirabhakaran) had failed . He hoped, no doubt, to undo the damage which India had done in training and arming the militants.

In the epic encounter that followed, the Indian army did its best to give effect to its government's policy and disarm the militant groups. It succeeded with all but the LTTE but that nut proved too much for them to crack. It was a re-run of the heroics of the David and Goliath story and a further repetition of the now-hackneyed theme of the vulnerability of conventional professional armies to guerillas fighting on their homeground. After two and a half years of fighting and heavy losses the IPKF created a local puppet organisation, the Tamil National Army, under the aegis of one of the militant groups — the Eelam People's Revolutionary Liberation Front (EPRLF) which, in an attempt to undermine the LTTE even made a unilateral declaration of independence of the state of Eelam. But by then the LTTE had reached the rapprochement with the new Sri Lankan government under President Premadasa described earlier. At the insistence of Premadasa the IPKF was withdrawn and the Indian central government's effort to achieve its first objective lay in shattered fragments around its feet. All chances of achieving a quasi-federal solution were now gone even if the Sri Lankan government were to accept one for there can be no federal arrangement with each of the federating states having an army of its own. The Indian central government still pays lip service to its first objective but it is now a mere spectator without effective leverage on either side. After the fall of Rajiv Gandhi's government in 1989 there has been a succession of weak minority governments at the centre in India with no alternative policy on the Sri Lanka problem.

The IPKF's presence in the northern and eastern provinces of Sri Lanka was disliked not only by the LTTE and most of the Sinhala people; it was also opposed by the state of Tamilnadu after fighting began between the IPKF and the LTTE. It is hard to conceive of a peace initiative that could have mustered such a coalition of diverse interests against it. Tamilnadu which had urged its central government to intervene militarily against the Sri Lankan government watched with chagrin the very opposite taking place. And when the IPKF finally withdrew from Sri Lanka the then chief minister of Tamilnadu registered his disapproval of the whole escapade by pointedly boycotting the welcoming ceremony for the returning troops.

The Indian general election of 1991 witnessed a high level of political turbulence throughout the country and Tamilnadu, where a state general election too took place simultaneously, was no exception. And it was in Tamilnadu that the dastardly assassination of Rajiv Gandhi took place. It is now certain that LTTE sympathisers whose families had suffered heavy casualties during the fighting between the IPKF and the LTTE were implicated in the suicide bombing assassination.

The Tamilnadu state election saw the rout of the ruling DMK and a landslide victory for the All India Anna DMK (AIADMK) led by former film actress Jayalalitha Jayaraman. The southern states of India were at that time strongly represented in high office at the centre. The President of India, Mr. R. Venkataraman, was a Tamil and the Prime Minister, Mr P.V. Narasimha Rao, is a politician from the Dravidian southern state of Andhra Pradesh which adjoins Tamilnadu to the north. The Jayalalitha government seeks to contain extreme Tamil nationalism by supporting the minority Congress government at the centre in return for its support in securing subordinate Tamil aspirations such as a fair apportionment of the waters of the Cauvery river (disputed by neighbouring Karnataka state) and the recovery of Kachchativu island from Sri Lanka. The latter has already roused apprehensions in Sri Lanka and there is little love lost between the two governments.

On the other hand Jayalalitha's opposition to the LTTE's presence in Tamilnadu is equally intense as the latter, more than any other entity, fans the flames of extreme Tamil nationalism and separatism in the state of Tamilnadu. She realises that the 230 refugee camps are hotbeds of nationalism and militarism with very unsettling effects on the local population. She has demanded that all the refugees be returned to Sri Lanka but the essential pre-requisite for this is a political settlement of the ethnic problem in the northeast of Sri Lanka. A military escalation there will result in the refugees being on her hands indefinitely. A major military effort by the Sri Lankan army to capture Jaffna and its peninsula for instance, is likely to generate a fresh flow of refugees into Tamilnadu compounding her problems. In such an event the probability is high that the LTTE will receive counterveiling support from Tamilnadu — if not overtly from its government, then covertly through non-official agents and organisations.

The other complication that muddies the South Asian waters is the Sri Lankan military establishment's links with their counterparts in Pakistan. There has been some officer training in Pakistan and, possibly, arms purchases there to a limited extent. If these links were to grow, however, there could be a resumption of support for the LTTE from the Indian central government perhaps through non-official Tamilnadu channels. It is a liaison to which the Indian central government is inordinately sensitive.

The final factor of note is the international impact of the Sri Lankan Tamil diaspora. A high proportion of the academic, professional and technically qualified personnel of the Tamil nation has fled to countries around the globe. A great number of them hold lucrative and responsible appointments in a variety of international, multi-national and national organisations. They have orchestrated the case, internationally, for an independent Tamil state, with great effect and have argued trenchantly against the manifest impossibility of achieving Sinhala-Tamil unity, let alone amity, by the use of force. The current pattern of ethnic wars accompanied by the emergence of new nation states — Ethiopia and Eritrea; Yugoslavia and Slovenia, Croatia, Bosnia-Herzegovina, Macedonia etc; the freeing of the three Baltic states from the forced embrace of the former Soviet Union and the break-up of the latter itself under nationalistic pressure — all these reinforce their impact on international opinion. They have well-organised cells in many key cities of the USA, UK, France, Germany, Australia to name but a few and now have long experience of mobilising financial and perhaps also military supplies for their cause. As the military dominance grows in Sri Lanka it will set off a concerted demand for international intervention.

A decisive and sustained military dominance in the Sinhala strategy will combine a host of reactive elements against it resulting possibly even in economic and military sanctions to end the carnage. These are risks that are better understood and dealt with in the civil domain rather than the military. They are unlikely to weigh equally heavily in military calculations based on the oft-repeated hopes of a quick and final victory. One does not have to reach far back in history for a great variety of cases which illustrate the point that guerilla wars of national liberation do not end that comfortably.

11

The Imperative of Peace

In the life of a nation, and in the lives of the individuals who make up a nation, nothing is more serious than war. Not only is it a matter of life and death; it is a matter of killing and being killed — a descent into bestiality which bespeaks a failure of rational, civilized intercourse and raises the most fundamental issues of public and private morality. It then becomes an inescapable necessity to judge the balance of morality as between the contending nations. So let us consider what this war is about.

For the Sinhala people and their government the war is being waged to preserve the territorial integrity of the country i.e. to preserve the territorial integrity of the colonial entity (Ceylon) which the British left to the successor government and which encompassed the whole of the island. Since war is deemed justifiable to preserve this entity we need to consider its nature.

In the British colony of Ceylon two nations — in colonial jargon termed "communities" as "nation" was too emotive and dangerous a word — were yoked together by the force of British arms. But they continued to occupy their historic homelands and their respective populations remained where they were and had been for centuries. The establishment of one political entity was for the British a matter of administrative convenience. There was no element of consultation with, or consent by, the two populations involved. The single entity was the result of an imperial fiat. It is that imperial fiat that the Sri Lankan government has decided to enforce; it is the entity resulting from that fiat that is to be preserved intact by this war.

The Tamil people, led by the LTTE, seek to establish a separate, independent, sovereign state for themselves comprising the area in which they form the majority of the population and which from historical times has held a largely Tamil population. This area comprises the northern and eastern provinces of the British colony of Ceylon which since 1987 have been merged into one north-east province. It is to establish a separate state in this area that the Tamil people voted overwhelmingly in the general election of 1977.

These are the two positions simply stated. And they give rise instantly to the question of on which side the balance of public morality lies. Is it right for the Sinhala people to insist on maintaining an entity created by an imperial fiat and thus inexorably reject the claim of the Tamil people? Is it right for the Tamil people to desire a separate state of their own which when established will inevitably split the imperial entity into two separate states?

To this writer, a Sinhala person with the moral integrity of the Sinhala people deeply at heart, the answers to these questions are self-evidently, unambiguously, clear. The Sinhala people have no imperial standing or right to enforce a former imperial master's fiat. They have not the right of conquest nor of imperial succession (i.e. they did not overthrow the British empire and siege its possessions). The Tamil people are fully justified in desiring a state of their own and likewise the Sinhala people are entitled to a state of their own.

The war that now rages is the result of the pseudo-imperial stand of the Sri Lankan government on the question of two states on the island. Prior to the British unification of the island into one state there were two or sometimes more states co-existing side-by-side on the island — not always peaceably but surviving as best they could. There is nothing inherently impossible in having two or even more states on an island which is nearly the size of the Netherlands, Belgium and Luxembourg combined. To go to war to preserve a colonial entity because it is larger than the Sinhala state that would emerge on separation is a *folie de grandeur* devoid of any moral justification. And moral justification is paramount in issues of war and peace.

Leaving aside for the moment the question of moral justification let us consider the question of expediency from the narrow point of view of the Sinhala people. The Sinhala people are a nation occupying a well-defined and uncontested part of the island i.e. the seven Sinhala provinces of the British colony, Ceylon. The colonial state — Ceylon — was not a nation state. It was, and is, a state in which two nations co-exist cheek by jowl — a multi-national, multi-ethnic, multi-religious, multi-cultural state. And the friction caused by the two nations being forced to live and move and have their being within the framework of a single state has proved too much for its legislators and its administrators alike. The Sinhala nation needs a state of its own in exactly the same way as the Tamil nation. To force the Sinhala nation into a multi-cultural state with ethnic quotas for everything thus focussing attention continuously on the ethnic divide is a grave disservice to the Sinhala nation and a recipe for disaster. What is needed between the two nations is amity not unity. The attempt to force unity has resulted in war not amity.

From the point of view of expediency the Sri Lankan government is embarked, and not for the first time, on a course which is the very opposite of what the Sinhala nation needs, which is a nation state of its own in which all who live within its bounds identify with the Sinhala people and consent to be governed within that state. Two nations seeking their destiny and fulfilment within their separate states are far more conducive to peace than the present manifestly absurd attempt to force unity by military means. What the use of armed force can secure, and has secured, is war not unity. The inherent nature of lasting unity is that it must needs be based on voluntary choice; voluntary choice and the compulsion of armed force are mutually exclusive. To believe they are compatible is repugnant to even the most elementary level of reason.

From the planes of morality and expediency let us now descend to that of practical possibility — the practical possibility of securing by force of arms the status quo ante 1983. That would require the total disarming of the LTTE, not just winning a battle or two. When President Premadasa commenced his dialogue with the LTTE in 1989 he stated openly, with a commendable grasp of reality, that disarming the LTTE was not a practical possibility. And that is why during the talks he sought to absorb the LTTE forces into Sri Lanka's military services. Nothing that has happened in the current phase of the war i.e. after June 1990 offers the slightest hope of the Sri Lankan army being able to disarm the LTTE.

Consider the nature of the war itself. The Sri Lankan army holds a few coastal outposts supplied by sea, a few camps within the north-east province supplied by helicopter and bases on the land boundary between the north-east province and the rest of the country. It sallies forth from these camps and fortifications during daytime, sweeps through an area within their range whence all opposition vanishes and by nightfall returns to its camps. The state of Eelam then rears its head in the selfsame area in the hours of darkness. On occasion the pattern is varied; the army advances in strength, overruns the LTTE's camps and bases and holds this ground for a time. As its extended lines suffer progressively from ambushes and guerilla harassment it withdraws once again to its camps and the captured ground reverts to the LTTE. It is a game that both sides can play ad infinitum.

The stark reality is that there can be no military victory until Tamil nationalism is extinguished. And there is little prospect of that. On the contrary, the war now raging has inflamed Tamil nationalism to a passionate level that has inspired the immense sacrifices now being made by the Tamil people as their volunteers for suicide missions so amply demonstrate.

The war has been represented to the Sinhala people not as a struggle of the Tamil people for independence — their overwhelming vote for a separate state in the 1977 general election is never referred to by press or politician — but as the result of the bloody-mindedness and wickedness of the LTTE and especially of its military commander Pirabhakaran. The capture or killing of this one man is an object of military strategy and is expected to end the war or to bring the LTTE to its knees and force it to sue for peace. A deeper analysis of the true causes of the war is either beyond the comprehension of the Sinhala leadership or, if comprehended, is deliberately withheld from the Sinhala public. Pirabhakaran is not the cause of Tamil nationalism; he is the result of it. If ever he is eliminated and achieves martyrdom in his nation's cause another equally determined military leader will take his place. Such men will not be scarce in the ranks of the LTTE's now battle-hardened military machine which is reckoned by international military analysts as one of the most formidable guerilla forces currently operating anywhere in the world.

The choice facing the Sinhala leadership is clear — peace with separation into two states or endless war.

The last straw of hope to which the Sinhala leadership clings is that the Tamil people are too war weary and cannot afford to sustain a long struggle. But who would have dreamt in 1983 that they could wage a war for eight years including two and a half years of relentless fighting with the Indian army? All the resources of man and woman power of the great majority of the Tamil people are committed to the conflict. They are not saddled with the costs of a conventional army nor the even more onerous burden of a civil government. They are able to fight on at a fraction of the cost it entails for the Sri Lankan government to fight this war. And support from the far-flung Tamil diaspora grows rather than diminishes with time. A nation with its back to the wall, fighting on its homeground, led by an unwavering leadership is unlikely to crumble from war-weariness.

On the contrary, the question is whether the Sri Lankan government can afford to continue this war burdened as it is with a costly social alleviation programme and a host of loss-making government corporations. The war now takes third place behind these priorities but when it begins to escalate and eat into the limited financial resources available the whole house of cards of the civil government could tumble. Indeed, the overblown civil government on the Sinhala side could well be a victim of the war long before the LTTE or Tamil nationalism.

So what is this expenditure of lives and treasure likely to produce for the Sinhala people? Nothing other than continuous war, an ever steeper descent into backwardness and impoverishment, a government teetering on the brink of collapsing into the embrace of the military and progressive isolation from, and ostracism by, the international community. The continuance of the war holds out no advantages or benefits whatsoever for the Sinhala people.

For them there is no rational option other than peace. But peace at what price?

12

The Cost of Peace

The peace of which the cost is to be discussed in this chapter is the peace that would result from the recognition by both nations of the existence of two states on the island — Sri Lanka comprising the seven Sinhala-occupied provinces of the former British colony of Ceylon and Eelam comprising the now-combined north-east province. Also this chapter considers the cost of peace from the point of view of the Sinhala people and not of the Tamil.

Perhaps the most important element of the cost of such a peace to the Sinhala people may be characterised as psychological. It covers a whole range of factors which need to be identified individually and considered dispassionately and rationally.

The first factor is the trauma of facing up to the realities of the situation. The Sinhala public has been carefully and deliberately shielded from them by the manipulation of the media by politicians playing to a chauvinist gallery. The true cause of the war — Tamil nationalism and the Sinhala government's decision to resist it — has not been clearly explained to the Sinhala people. The impossibility of the Sri Lankan army winning a guerilla war fought on the homeground of the Tamil people has never been suggested even as a remote contingency. The enormous cost of the war to the Sri Lankan government in purely financial terms has never been divulged; only the guestimates of foreign academics and journalists give some inkling to the few readers who have access to the foreign publications which carry them. These realities have never been disclosed as to do so would lead to widespread misgivings about the wisdom of the Sri Lankan government's policy. Their disclosure, with the accompanying shock it will entail for a people who have been kept for years in a fool's paradise, will be one factor in the psychological cost of peace for the Sinhala people.

The second factor in the psychological area is the entire concept of "giving" something to the Tamil people — in this case one-third of "our land". The Sinhala discussion of the Tamil people's aspirations is always couched in terms of a demand by "them" for something from "us". "They want our land and we are not going to give it to them." Sinhala politicians, the Sinhala press, Buddhist religious leaders — all have consistently used this frame of reference. The Sinhala people have not the slightest inkling of the fact that the Tamil people want nothing from them. The Tamil people are in possession of their homeland, they live there already (having done so for centuries) and all they want is to establish for themselves a state of their own in that homeland. In order to do so they are waging war to expel the Sinhala army from their state. The Sinhala people are not called upon to give anything to the Tamil people. A recognition that the Tamil nation owns the homeland in which they live is merely a recognition of a self-evident reality. It is not an act of giving or sacrifice by the Sinhala people — one cannot give to others what already belongs to them. It is essential to peace that the Sinhala consciousness should be changed to accept the true nature of the situation and that the misguided idea of "giving up" or "sacrificing" a part of "our territory" should itself be given up.

The third psychological factor is the mythical insecurity of the Sinhala people — going back to king Dutugemunu who is said to have felt boxed in by the Tamils in the north and the sea in the south and thus could not stretch himself to the fullest. A latter day variant of this complex is that the Sinhala people have nowhere else to go whereas the Tamil people always have a home-base in India. A further variant of this theme is that the Sinhala people are really a minority compared to the neighbouring Tamil people including the Tamil population of the Indian state of Tamilnadu. All these are emotive ideas expressed by Sinhala leaders (who ought to know better) from time to time. And, however absurd, they do form part of the Sinhala psyche and give a sense of justification to the war. But none of them bear rational examination. Nobody is threatening to expel the Sinhala people from the territory in which they have lived for centuries and to drive them into the sea. The English do not entertain the fear that the Scots in the north will rise and drive the entire English population en masse into the Atlantic. Such fantasies are not consistent with even the most elementary level of sanity and they are unworthy of a people such as the Sinhala who have had a long and civilized history. Equally nonsensical is the bogey that the Sinhala nation has nowhere to go to but the Tamil people have India. The first characteristic of a nation is that it is rooted to its territory. Nations do not pull up the stakes and march en masse into another country. There is no call on the Sinhala people to go anywhere; the territory in which they have lived for centuries has sufficed perfectly well for them and in many respects they are very fortunate in its possession. They should rejoice in it and prosper with its many resources instead of hallucinating about "nowhere else to go". And most fantastic of all is the minority complex. It is perfectly true that the Tamil race, taken as a whole, is more numerous than the Sinhala and also that they are cheek by jowl. The whole world is covered by such juxtapositions. The many countries whose borders march with China are in this position; so also with the neighbours of the United States; the Poles are wedged in between the Germans and the Russians. Indeed the juxtaposition of small nations with big ones is the rule rather than the exception and calls not for hysterical alarm and dismay but for sensible good-neighbourly policies. No Sinhala politician or leader has tried to dispel these atavistic fears and many have played on them to draw support for their chosen ethnic strategy.

In the modern world the security of small nations is not as precarious as in former times. The recent Gulf war was fought to punish aggression against a small country and to restore it to independence. (Cynics claimed it was to safeguard Kuwait's oil for the world, but the world has managed well enough without the oil of both Kuwait and Iraq). The will of the comity of nations in maintaining orderly international relationships is what small countries need to foster. Both Sri Lanka and Eelam will have a vested interest in supporting international mediation and peacekeeping efforts.

To create the climate needed to turn the Sinhala people towards peace it is essential that these psychological cobwebs should be dusted off the Sinhala psyche and that they be encouraged to confront the world of reality with clear-eyed confidence.

Apart from the psychological factors, the Sinhala people will have to face up to more tangible problems as well. It is these that will be addressed in the following paragraphs.

The first of these is that around a quarter of a milllion Sinhala people living in the state of Eelam will, for the first time, have a minority status. From being members of a majority they will become a minority and reasonable apprehensions as to their future are bound to arise. When the French government under de Gaulle withdrew from Algeria leaving behind in that country a population of a million ethnic French people, the same apprehensions arose. But there was an even larger number of ethnic Algerians already settled in France. The existence of a minority of each nation residing in the other has made for moderation and reasonableness in the treatment of the minority by each government. The earlier precedent of the separation of the Irish Republic from Great Britain had witnessed the same problem of a minority of one nation dwelling in the other and there too the apprehensions proved unfounded. The situation is the same as between Sri Lanka and Eelam — each will contain a minority of people from the other state and that will make for reciprocal moderation and reasonableness in the treatment of the minority.

There is then the question of the Muslims who are resident in both states. Those resident in the state of Eelam were unavoidably caught up in the war and those of them who supported the Sinhala forces were attacked by the LTTE and defended by the Sri Lankan army. Unlike the Sinhala people the Muslims have a centuries-long experience of minority status wherever they lived. There is no reason to believe that in the state of Eelam, to which they have the affinity of language, they will fare any worse than in the state of Sri Lanka.

The general question of the treatment of minorities after separation will be discussed in the next chapter on the nature of peace.

The second area of tangible cost to the Sinhala people derives from the fact that one-third of the land area and two-thirds of the coastline of the island will no longer be in the state of Sri Lanka.

As regards the land area its potential for resettlement of landless Sinhala peasant farmers disappeared when war broke out. Indeed such resettlement was one of the proximate causes of the war. However, there still are undeveloped areas in the Southern, Uva and Sabaragamuwa provinces capable of development for resettlement and peace will release funds for the purpose. Furthermore, the undeniable fact that opportunities for developing presently undeveloped land are limited and will soon be exhausted will serve as strong impetus for more intensive and scientific cultivation of already cultivated land with prospects of a very favourable cost-benefit relationship.

In regard to the coastline falling in the state of Eelam, it is seasonally migrant Sinhala fishermen who could be affected. It is very unlikely that their operations will be stopped by the new state of Eelam as the fish catch is sold partly in local markets and so is beneficial to the local people. However, the activities of these fishermen may be regulated and some licensing fees and taxes could be levied from them. Such imposts inevitably find their way to the final purchasers of the product through the pricing system so the net adverse effect on the fishermen themselves is likely to be marginal.

The final element of tangible costs to the Sinhala people relates to the division of the infrastructure and services that now cover the whole island. The railways, electricity, telecommunication, and irrigation networks fall within this area. The division of moveable and fixed assets as well as on-going operation and pricing of products and services traded between the two states will have to be dealt with.

In the area of services, the apportionment of personnel in various branches of the public service between the two states and an agreement on liability to pensions obligations proportionate to the period of service under each state will have to be negotiated. This will apply also to the sharing of the national debt to both local and foreign creditors.

All these are matters on which there exists already a whole range of precedents and quite a galaxy of experienced international personnel whose advice and mediatory services should be secured and paid for by both states. The separation of the Irish Republic from Great Britain is a good but now rather distant precedent. A more recent and relevant experience is the separation of India and Pakistan and both these countries will undoubtedly assist by providing experienced and impartial chairmen for the joint commissions that will have to be established for each sector of the common infrastructure. The European Community has now built up much expertise in the operation of a common infrastructure spanning the nine contiguous countries of the community (excluding the Irish Republic, Great Britain and Greece) and the United Nations itself could help in securing the necessary technical assistance especially in the apportionment of debts to the International Monetary Fund, the World Bank and the Asian Development Bank as well as to the countries of the Paris Consortium.

All of the foregoing are matters of immediate importance at the point of separation. They should not blind us, however, to the more long-term costs to the Sinhala people. These may be encapsulated in the term *lebensraum* or room for expansion. It is a problem for Sri Lanka rather for Eelam where the ratio of population to land will be favourable. Sri Lanka will be in a more difficult position. It will have an initial population of around 15 million people in a land area comparable to that of the Netherlands which too has 15 million people. But Sri Lanka's rate of population growth is higher than that of most European countries (it is nearly double that of the Netherlands) and it contains elements, such as the Tamil plantation-worker population, which have a high growth rate. There will unquestionably be a need to tackle urgently the population problem on two fronts — first, to reduce growth trends in all sectors of the population and secondly, to promote vigorously policies for emigration for employment. The educational system should be outwardly focused, weighted for language and technical skills and linked to the educational systems of target countries. A much wider horizon for emigration should be adopted, adding to the Middle East countries, the newly-emerging Asian Republics of the former Soviet Union, South Africa and Latin American countries, especially those which have already absorbed an early wave of Japanese immigrants (Brazil, Peru). There will be, undoubtedly, some emigration from the plantation Tamil population to Eelam as the latter grows in prosperity and begins to feel the shortage both of labour and of skills. Peace will enable Sri Lanka to re-join the world as a provider of skilled and efficient professionals and technicians and not as a source of penniless and desperate refugees.

So far in this chapter the cost of peace to the Sinhala people has been considered. It is now time to turn to the benefits they may reasonably expect.

In the area of costs the intangible, psychological costs were regarded as perhaps the most important and difficult. So it is also in the area of benefits. In the view of this writer the most important benefit of all, the one which overrides all others, is that peace with separation will rescue the Sinhala people from the calamity of engaging in a war in which the moral balance is not on their side. It is the direst fate that any nation can suffer and those nations that have suffered it cannot lightly wash their guilt away. Within living memory some of today's greatest nations have undergone this trauma — Germany in the first and especially in the second World War, Japan in the second World War, the USA in Vietnam, the former Soviet Union in Afghanistan. The knowledge of having engaged in an unjust war brings with it a pain and a guilt that affects the psyche of these nations and informs the work of their most sensitive writers both now and for generations to come. The Tamil nation on the island is entitled to a state of their own comprising the homeland in which they live. The effort of the Sinhala people, misled by all their governments, to deny the Tamil people that right and to crush that aspiration by military force is nakedly immoral, and for that reason foredoomed to failure. That they should cease and desist from such culpable folly will be for them the greatest benefit of peace. In the paragraphs that follow, the enormous material and financial benefits that peace will bring to the Sinhala people will be delineated. All of them put together can never equal the moral deliverance that peace will afford them.

Of the tangible benefits of peace, the first will be a sharp reduction in military expenditure which will provide funds for upgrading the woefully inadequate and antiquated infrastructure in Sri Lanka. After 48 years of independence the country has not a single mile of motorway or "A" class road (with a central division and two lanes on either side); not a single mile of electrified railroad; not a single city with underground transport; an overwhelming majority of the population unsupplied with potable water or electricity; an educational system which in quality lags far behind that of many comparable countries. Every area of public life needs modernisation and even the money saved from military expenditure will be but a drop in the ocean of need. Peace will enable the first significant steps to be taken.

There will also be an immediate reduction in administrative and social welfare costs resulting from separation. Administrative costs are set to increase sharply with the introduction of a fresh new tier of local government — the provincial councils. The hiving off of the north-east will mitigate this increase. During the years of warfare hardly any tax revenues would have been forthcoming from the north-east. On the other hand the payment of salaries to government servants living and working in that area (and likely as not carrying out the LTTE's orders as much as those of the government) is a net drain which will be saved by peace.

The contraction of area will produce savings in infrastructure maintenance costs — on roads, railways, telecommunications, hospitals, schools etc.. These savings could be used to upgrade the same facilities in the new state of Sri Lanka.

Both states will be able to benefit from cross-border trading with each other as against overseas exports with all their attendant problems and delays. This is a great benefit which the continental EC countries enjoy in their trade with each other and from which Britain is partly excluded by its physical separation from the continent.

Peace itself and the inevitable rising tide of prosperity will together engender a reverse braindrain — both of nationals returning home bringing with them the capital, expertise and above all contacts acquired during their sojourn abroad as well as of foreign experts, financiers, investors etc. attracted by the pent-up demand for their services that will be released.

And finally, there will be a surge in foreign investment on a scale that people in Sri Lanka have not even dared contemplate if the right policies to attract it are in place. The capital needs of the country are such that nothing but foreign equity investment can meet them. With that secured Sri Lanka can look forward to making the great leap that is necessary to join the newly industrialising countries of the region by the end of this century.

Peace will transform all the hitherto known parameters of development and lift Sri Lanka and its people to a level of prosperity undreamt of up to now.

A realistic and comprehensive assessment of the costs and benefits of peace to the Sinhala people and their government is important and that is what has been attempted in this chapter. But even more important is the relationship between the two states and their attitude towards each other for that will determine the nature of the peace between them.

13

The Nature of Peace

It is a hackneyed, but true saying that peace is not the mere absence of war. An armed truce is not peace and as such an arrangement will not last. It is extremely important, therefore, that right from the beginning a positive and rewarding relationship of cooperation and mutual understanding and assistance should be consciously fostered by both states. There is now a historic opportunity for Eelam, which has suffered so many disappointments in its relationships with both the Indian central government and the state government of Tamilnadu, to turn to Sri Lanka. For the Sinhala government of Sri Lanka too there is now a historic opportunity to take the initiative in recognising the state of Eelam — a step which the Indian central government has refused consistently to take in its own self-interest and which all the governments of Tamilnadu state too have shrunk from for fear of alienating the centre. With the abandonment of the inherently flawed policy of trying to secure unity by military force, the quest for amity could be pursued in an atmosphere far more conducive to success.

The preceding chapter referred to the "peace dividend". The saving in military expenditure resulting from the cessation of military operations will be considerable; but even more important in the long run are the benefits of running down the military establishments of both countries to the lowest level consistent with domestic law and order requirements for which the armed services are the final reserve.

On the all too rare occasions when peace with separation is mentioned, even as a remote possibility, the rational discussion of it is stifled by a reference to two factors which are assumed, sui generis, to guarantee future discord and conflict. They are bound-

BOUNDARIES

The existing boundary between the seven predominantly Sinhala-occupied provinces of the former colony of Ceylon — the provinces and their boundaries were established under British rule — and the now-combined north-east province is a clear and recognised one. The wisest and most practicable course is to adopt this boundary between the two states of Sri Lanka and Eelam. In the pre-colonial history of the island i.e. upto the beginning of the sixteenth century, when several feudal kingdoms and overlordships existed side-by-side, conflicts over territory were the rule. During the Portuguese and Dutch colonial periods too, when at least two states and many local overlords held sway over territory, wars between them erupted frequently. It is only in the relatively short period of 168 years from 1815 to 1983 that territorial conflict was absent. But the past of turmoil is deeply embedded in the Sinhala psyche and the conviction is universal that the border between the two states will be fought over once again. There is a constantly-voiced medieval, feudal fear that "they" will encroach on, or even openly invade, "our" land.

On the continental land masses of the world, land borders are common and have been a source of friction and war. But by and large they have tended to stabilise and to be accepted by the nations whose countries are bounded by them. The division of islands between two or more states is less common and most island nations have the certitude of the sea as their boundary. But exceptions there are, and they span the whole gamut of size. The island of Cyprus is very small — about one-eighth the size of Sri Lanka — and it is now divided between two states, the Greek Cypriot Republic and the Turkish Cypriot Republic with the boundary between them patrolled by a United Nations peace-keeping force of international composition. The Caribbean island of Hispaniola, which is slightly bigger than Ceylon, is divided between two states — the Dominican Republic (the bigger) and Haiti (the smaller). There have been no border problems between them. Next up the ladder of scale is the land of the mother of parliaments itself, Great Britain, which was one unitary state encompassing the whole of the British Isles up to 1922 when it split into two unitary states — The Republic of Ireland (at the inception called The Irish Free State) and the United (!) Kingdom of Great Britain and Northern Ireland. The boundary that was adopted between the two states was the existing boundary between the counties that fell into each state. The same misgivings about the sanctity of this boundary were then entertained in Britain as are now common in Sri Lanka. But for the 70 years since Irish independence it has served the two states well and has not been a source of conflict. On the large island of Borneo there are three states — a part of Indonesia, a part of Malaysia and the independent kingdom of Brunei and here too the boundaries have not been fought over. So also in the largest of all the divided islands — New Guinea — which is divided between the Indonesian state of Irian Jaya and the independent, sovereign state of Papua New Guinea. And there too the boundary has not been a problem.

There is no reason whatsoever for the boundary between the two states of Sri Lanka and Eelam on the island of Ceylon to be any different from the examples of divided island states given above. On the other hand the boundary could provide an opportunity for sensible, humane and cooperative policies by both states which establish a foundation of goodwill and good-neighbourliness between them.

For instance, since it would be impossible to regulate the crossing and re-crossing of the border along every inch of it, there could be the minimum of supervision and no visa requirements at all at the established, existing road-crossings. Such is the case today between the UK and the Irish Republic and also within the three Benelux countries.

The same freedom could apply to residence on a reciprocal basis. Today citizens of the Irish Republic can live freely in Great Britain and vice versa and the same is true of the Benelux countries. A subject of any of the three kingdoms in that union can reside freely in any of the other two. Citizens of Sri Lanka and Eelam should enjoy the same facility. All that is required is that they should be subject to the laws of the state of domicile.

The boundary should not be used to impede trade between the two states. There should be no tariff nor quota restrictions between them nor duties levied either as export or import duties on goods and services traded between them. This is the case between the UK and the Irish Republic and between the Benelux countries.

The boundary should not hamper corporate enterprise on either side of it. Companies in one state should be eligible to bid for and to perform work, both public and private, in the other without any boundary restrictions to curtail their scope. It is now well-known that though countries tend to separate and stay separate, market gravitate towards coalesence and unity.

Thus a cooperative, humane and sensible attitude by both states towards boundary issues could be the beginning of amity and peace between them. Peace will then have a real content in which each state has a vested interest.

MINORITIES

This is a sensitive but by no means insuperable problem. Indeed, as in the case of the boundary it provides a great opportunity for both states to influence for good the quality of peace between them.

In the demonizing hysteria of war-time it is not uncommon for Sinhala people to say "The Tamils live among us and have it so good, but they have driven our people out of the north-east". All such emotive outbursts have some degree of truth and an even larger degree of paranoia. It is perfectly true that large numbers of Tamil people, of all social classes, live in towns in the Sinhala area. Hardly any are in Sinhala villages. They have had a rough ride in the 27-year period from 1956 to 1983 with regular pogroms against them culminating in the "holocaust" of July 1983. The international repercussions of that final horror shook the Sinhala leadership and since then there have been no attacks on the Tamil population living in Sinhala towns. And as for the Tamils themselves they have stayed on — and some who fled in 1983 to their homes in the north-east or even to India have come back — because they have established businesses or careers to pursue. They have had some reassurance from the fact that even during the height of the attacks on them there were Sinhala people who sheltered and protected them. They cannot, and do not, tar the whole Sinhala nation with one brush.

As for the driving out of Sinhala people from the north-east there is some truth in that too but the attendant circumstances are illuminating. In a great many of the "colonization schemes" i.e. resettlement schemes for landless people, in the north-east the "colonists" that the government put in were mostly Sinhala people drawn from the overcrowded Sinhala areas. There was a relatively smaller number of Tamil colonists too. The policy of introducing

Sinhala colonists into predominantly Tamil areas (there was no reciprocal policy of introducing Tamil colonists into predominantly Sinhala areas) was vigorously opposed by all the elected Tamil MPs but without success. In some areas the Sinhala influx was so large that the ethnic composition of the population was transformed in favour of the Sinhala newcomers. When war broke out it is these Sinhala newcomers who felt the heat and quit their homesteads for the safety of refugee camps under the control of the Sinhala government. To that extent there has been an expulsion of Sinhala people from the north-east.

There is, however, an indigenous Sinhala population especially in the former eastern province. These people remain and have not been expelled though those suspected of collaboration with the Sinhala army have been attacked by the LTTE from time to time. They, however, remain a minority in Eelam just like the Eelam Tamil minority in Sri Lanka.

The treatment of minorities has bedevilled politics in Ceylon and Sri Lanka from the very first year of independence. We have seen in earlier chapters how the Tamil plantation-worker minority was grossly discriminated against and rendered both stateless and voteless by a Sinhala-dominated parliament. All that has happened since then has taught both the Sinhala public and its leaders that the treatment of minorities is not merely a question of majority rule which the minority has perforce to "like it or lump it". The consent of the governed, which is the bedrock on which democratic government − or even a near approximation to it − rests cannot be secured by force. And its withdrawal by a whole minority can have devastating social and political consequences. The rights of minorities, *as perceived by themselves* set very specific limits to the majority's freedom of action. The Sri Lankan experience has driven home that lesson in no uncertain terms. Not only has the discriminatory legislation been reversed but it is very unlikely that any such folly will be perpetrated in future. The pronouncements of the LTTE on the question of minority rights in Eelam also augur well for the future.

Sri Lanka, in its new configuration after separation and peace, will have three distinct ethnic minorities. First, there will be the Tamil people of Eelam origin who either opt for Sri Lankan citizenship or take Eelam citizenship. Second, the Tamil plantation-worker population all now Sri Lankan citizens and third, the Muslims all of whom are Sri Lankan citizens. The first and last are scattered throughout Sri Lanka in urban locations and are present in every one of the seven provinces. The second, the plantation-worker Tamil population, is concentrated in the plantation districts where their very concentration affords them a real opportunity, which they are now beginning to avail of, of effective participation in local government and politics.

All of them, including the Muslims, are Tamil-speaking, so Tamil will have to continue as an official language in Sri Lanka. And English, which is the language of the middle class which spans all ethnic divides, too will have to have the same status.

In the state of Eelam there is no plantation-Tamil presence so there will be only two minorities — Sinhala and Muslim. Both are in compact areas in the former eastern province. There are smaller concentrations of Muslims in the former northern province too. This concentration enables them, like the plantation-Tamil population in Sri Lanka, to participate effectively in local government and politics. It is very much to be hoped that the state of Eelam will be democratically organised so that the minorities could be represented in its legislature. Here too, English as the language of the middle class of all three ethnic elements should be an official language of the state along with Tamil and Sinhala.

From the beginning of British rule up to the present the personal laws of the minorities — the Thesawalamai of the Tamil and the Wakf of the Muslims — have been recognized and applied to them in the normal courts. This enlightened policy will no doubt continue to be observed in the two states.

We come finally to three areas in which minority rights can become very sensitive and contentious issues — education, the media and religion.

In education the right of an ethnic minority to preserve and foster its language by having it as a medium of instruction for their children in the state schools has been recognized and applied in Sri Lanka. For financial and other reasons the majority has been better served in this respect than the minorities. Nevertheless, the principle should be entrenched in both states; and there is here a great area for cooperation between them in respect of language teaching, especially in securing an adequate supply of qualified teachers for the different language streams. At the university level such cooperation could extend to the exchange of students and faculty in rotation. Such a relationship in the academic field could have a great influence in modifying the mutual perception of each other's national characters and in laying to rest the hysterical demonology that the war has engendered on both sides.

An equally vital area is the media — both printed and electronic. The enormous damage that the Sinhala leaders have done to their nation by their refusal to tolerate a totally free and untrammelled press and broadcast service is now widely acknowledged. No modern state can function effectively without both in times of war as well as in times of peace. It is for lack of both that Tamil nationalism has not been understood by the Sinhala people and that a separation that could conceivably have been achieved in peace and in an orderly manner has had to be forced by war and all its attendant horrors. Peace affords an opportunity for a total reversal of this deluded and self-destructive policy and both states should start with a tabula rasa in this field. Journalists and media crew of each state should be made welcome in the other so that the coexistence of the two states side-by-side could be in an atmosphere of glasnost and perestroika. Freedom of the media is vital for healing the wounds of war and elevating the nature of peace to the enlightened, humanitarian level that both nations require after the miasma of unnecessary conflict.

The third sensitive area is religion; for the sacred shrines of Tamil Hindus (there are no Tamil Buddhists) and Sinhala Buddhists (there are no Sinhala Hindus) and Muslims are scattered over both states. Complete and untrammelled freedom of access to these shrines, the making of endowments and designated gifts to them, the residence of the clergy of the respective religions at these shrines and security for, and freedom of worship by the public of both states at them should be guaranteed irrevocably and widely publicised. Both Sinhala and Tamil people are deeply religious and are bound to turn ever more fervently to their religions when peace comes to salve the pain and suffering they have endured during this fratricidal conflict. It should be high on the agenda of each state on the arrival of peace to nurture these oases of healing for all the people of either state. The nature of peace can be enriching and renewing only if it is inspired by forgiveness and repentance.

The two nations have worked assiduously at war and the Tamil people have made enormous sacrifices to achieve a tangible, material goal. To make the peace worthwhile even greater application and assiduity are required. It may be even more difficult for the Tamil people than for the Sinhala for they will have to turn from a concrete, specific, clearly-recognisable goal to a more intangible one. Both nations have to learn that peace and its rewards are far more estimable and far more devoutly to be desired than the fruits of war.

14

The Continuance of Peace

The three preceding chapters have dealt with the imperative of peace for the Sinhala people, its costs and benefits from their point of view, and what opportunities are likely to be available for developing an amicable and co-operative relationship between the two states once peace has been achieved. It is time now to turn to the question of how to make such a peace an enduring one. After a centuries-long history of conflict, suspicion and distrust between the two peoples there is now a historic opportunity to end that dark and horrendous past and emerge into a new day of enlightened, civilized, humane relationships based on mutual respect. Every endeavour must be made to ensure that this new phase in the relationship between the two nations should be a lasting one.

Once again the first bridge to cross is psychological. It is important that both sides should regard each other as equals despite the disparity in size; that neither is a winner or loser of the war; that each has a right to an independent existence in a nation state of its own. Such a change in mutual perception is essential to enshrine the principle of reciprocity in all dealings between them. The atmosphere of reciprocity is the best environment for developing rational, mutually beneficial relationships. It will nip in the bud any hint of pressure or threat, either of which could easily tip the two sides on to the downward slope of confrontation and renewed war. Reciprocity at every level of the relationship is the first priority.

The second, which is important in the immediate aftermath of the war, is the reduction of the armed might of both states. This has necessarily to be negotiated and a balanced and verifiable programme of reductions agreed on. Scrapping of existing armaments acquired by both sides at great cost may not be practicable. If so, they could be phased out by obsolescence and non-replacement. Any future upgrading of military capability should be agreed on and should be mutually verifiable in order to eliminate suspicion and engender a climate of trust. The fruits of peace could easily be jeopardised by an arms race and both sides should do their utmost to avert that calamity.

Whereas the reduction of military hardware presents problems, the running down of military personnel is easier. Here too an agreed and mutually verifiable programme of retrenchment should be negotiated.

Another area of immediate concern on the arrival of peace is the return of Tamil refugees from Tamilnadu. The Indian central government, the government and people of Tamilnadu state and the international community will undoubtedly help in every aspect of this enormous task. The government of Sri Lanka should be foremost among them not with the intent of winning hearts and minds or influencing the internal politics of Eelam but as a simple act of restitution and human solidarity with neighbours in need.

Likewise the return of Sinhala refugees to their former homes in Eelam should be effected with the cooperation of both states.

When the war is over the stage will be set for the state of Eelam to repair its damaged relationships with the Indian central government and with the state of Tamilnadu. Similarly, the state of Sri Lanka too will have the opportunity of building up with both these entities new relationships based on mutual respect and friendship and of ending the long period of discord and suspicion.

Neither Sri Lanka nor Eelam should seek to drive a wedge between the other and the two Indian entities. All four parties will have a historic opportunity for setting the past behind them and embarking on a new era of friendship, cooperation and peace. Policies based on this perception of their four-cornered relationship will go a long way towards ensuring a lasting peace.

With the emergence of Eelam as a separate state, Sri Lanka could, and should, assist in its entry into the United Nations Organisation and other international agencies. The Indian Government may find such an initiative difficult for itself for reasons of domestic self-interest but will undoubtedly support a Sri Lankan initiative. Steps such as this to smoothen the way for the entry of the fledgling state onto the international arena will lay the foundations for lasting goodwill.

From what is necessary in the immediate aftermath of war and from the external policies needed to secure a lasting peace we must turn now to the area of bilateral relations between the two states and to a consideration of what policies are needed to ensure the continuance of that peace.

Human beings being what they are it is very unlikely that on every issue that arises between the two states negotiations will result in agreement. It is very important, therefore, that both sides should determine at the very outset that all such disagreements should be settled by international arbitration and that the arbitrator's award should be binding on both states. The hackneyed objection that the availability of arbitration will promote intransigence by both sides is illusory as the prospect of the binding award of an arbitrator going against one or the other will be a spur to finding a mutually acceptable solution among themselves if that were at all possible. In matters that fall within the purview of the International Court of Justice in The Hague both sides should agree to seeking its mediation and to being bound by its awards.

Another area in which enlightened policies will have a far-reaching effect in securing a lasting peace is that of minorities. Each state should forswear, from the very outset, any intention of setting itself up as the guardian or protector of their ethnic minority in the other state. As a corollary of this policy each state should do nothing to cause disaffection between its ethnic minority in the other state and the government of that state. Specifically, the Sri Lankan government should not consider that it has any rights or duties in respect of the Sinhala (and also Muslim) minority in the state of Eelam. It must take on board the fact that its only influence on the state of Eelam is the enlightened and generous treatment of the Eelam Tamil and plantation-worker Tamil minorities in the state of Sri Lanka.

Likewise, the state of Eelam should cut its links with the Eelam Tamil, plantation-worker Tamil and Muslim populations in Sri Lanka and seek their good in that state by adopting towards the Sinhala and Muslim minorities in Eelam enlightened, humane and considerate policies.

The golden rule of "do as you would be done by" should be the basis of the minority policies of each state. There is little doubt that the presence of an ethnic minority of each state's population in the other will serve as the best guarantee of the equitable and just treatment of minorities in both states. It is, nevertheless, a sensitive area and one in which a completely new departure has to be made by each state. A vigilant monitoring of minority sensitivities, with generous intent in their treatment, will usher in a new quality of life in each state and that in turn will be conducive to enduring peace.

Another necessary determination at the outset is non-interference in each other's domestic politics. Here the record so far augurs well. From the general election of 1977 when no Sinhala political party contested a seat in the northern province there has been little opportunity for Sinhala intervention in Eelam politics. The conflict between the LTTE and the other Tamil political parties and militant groups was an internecine affair with no Sinhala intervention. Indeed Sinhala support for any Tamil political party would have amounted to a kiss of death for such a party. Conversely, the LTTE has exerted no political influence in Sri Lanka. Its links with the JVP were at best tenuous and could never have amounted to much on account of the JVP's hysterical xenophobia. And more recently when President Premadasa was accused of treason in supplying weapons to the LTTE, the latter who could provide proof positive one way or the other has chosen not to throw an apple of discord into the Sinhala political melee. It is vital for a long-lasting peace that both sides should adopt an irrevocable policy of non-interference in each other's domestic politics. Rather should they compete to be ever more truly democratic and liberal and humane than the other.

The nitty-gritty of bilateral relations is not unimportant in fostering a lasting peace. There ought to be regular meetings of Heads of State and senior ministers, officials and service chiefs. We have seen earlier, in Chapter 12, the need for joint commissions for operating the common infrastructure. There will have to be a double taxation agreement and an extradition treaty for criminal offences, on both of which the British-Irish arrangements could be useful precedents to follow. There will need to be close collaboration between the police, customs and excise authorities of the two states. It is these working relationships that will reassure both states of each other's good intentions and of their determination to coexist side by side in a co-operative and friendly atmosphere. The end of the quest for a forced unity will pave the way for a successful march towards amity.

There is a strong presumption that both states will be constitutional democracies with an elected legislature. In view of the certainty of a very considerable mobility of people, especially workers, between the two states agreement will have to be reached as to their voting rights. As is now the well-established international practice, permanent residents should have voting rights in the state of permanent domicile irrespective of citizenship. Thus citizens of Eelam who are permanently resident in Sri Lanka should have their voting rights in Sri Lanka and not in Eelam and vice versa. This is important to secure the principle of "no taxation without representation" and so strengthen the democratic foundations of both states. And that in turn will enhance the prospects of a lasting peace.

Both states can take comfort from the facts of history in that there are precedents to follow. The one precedent on all fours with theirs is the separation of the Irish Free State (now The Republic of Ireland) from the United Kingdom in 1922. There will be much to learn from that experience for that separation ended centuries of unrest and guerilla warfare and secured a peace which has lasted for 70 years despite almost universal scepticism at the time that separation would bring about such a result. However, it contains a warning of the greatest importance. The retention of Northern Ireland within the United Kingdom in order for the latter to protect the Protestant population of that area (largely non-Irish descendants of Scottish and English settlers in that part of Ireland) has resulted in continuing strife and bloodshed and urban guerilla warfare with no prospect of peace in sight. It is a precedent that has a direct bearing on the former eastern province of Ceylon where there is a mixed population. It will be a recipe for certain disaster if the Sinhala government of Sri Lanka attempts to hive-off from Eelam either the whole of the eastern province or that part of it which is Sinhala-occupied and make it a part of Sri Lanka. The seeds of certain war in the future will be sown by such a policy. Bismarck once said very truly that "only fools learn by experience; the wise man learns from the experience of others." It is a saying that is very apposite to the point at issue. The government of Sri Lanka must not repeat the grave and costly mistake made by the British in 1922 in respect of Northern Ireland.

And, finally, there is another precedent that the two states can, in the fullness of time, follow — and it too is from a former imperial power in Ceylon — that of the Dutch in the Benelux Union. That Union was a precursor of the Treaty of Rome which set up the European Economic Community and the Dutch have acquired a wealth of experience in the pragmatic arrangements necessary for the successful working of such a Union. It is true to say, however, that it is the complete and total sovereign independence enjoyed by the three states of the Netherlands, Belgium and Luxembourg for many years that has enabled them to make voluntarily the mutual accommodations necessary for such a Union. Such a Union is essentially voluntary and cannot be secured by the use of force.

If ever such a Union becomes possible on the island of Ceylon it will only be after years of complete and total separation and sovereign independence. When both sides have had enough reassurance of the other's respect and goodwill then, and only then, will they be in a position to take the voluntary steps that could result in such a Union. So, paradoxically, total separation is an essential prerequisite for the will to take the voluntary steps towards Union.

It is in the best interests of both states actively to keep in touch with Irish and British governments on the one hand and the Benelux Union on the other, to learn from them how separation followed by cooperation can work successfully. The total independence and sovereignty of the state of Eelam that is the be-all and end-all of the LTTE and the sovereignty of the nation-state of Sri Lanka after separation need not necessarily be the "end of history" for them. After the passage of time and the healing of the wounds of war they could well discover that it is in their best interests to join voluntarily in the Union of "Srilam."

15

How to Get There

In the 48 years since independence in 1948, political evolution in Sri Lanka has been remarkable for its volatility. There have been radical constitutional changes — from monarchy to republic, from a bicameral to a unicameral legislature, from "first-past-the-post" elections to proportional representation, from a Westminster style of cabinet government to a presidential form of cabinet government, from one elected sovereign legislature to two directly elected centres of power — the legislature and the president. In comparison with the relative inertia of other, especially neighbouring countries the pace of constitutional change in Sri Lanka has been positively frenetic. And these changes were not effected in response to a groundswell of public demand; they were elitist options accepted by the public with a bemused apathy.

The case is the same in the domain of policies, except here public interest has been very lively. Every sacred cow exalted in the name of the "welfare of the people", especially of the Sinhala people, has been slain as we shall soon see. It is not too far-fetched to say that the public is innured now to radical change. Complete somersaults in policy are accepted by the public if not with nonchalance at least with a sullen resignation.

In Chapter 7 the volte-face of July 1987 by President Jayawardene was evaluated in respect of its implications for the war and for the relationship with India. It has equally important implications for domestic (i.e. Sinhala) politics and these we shall examine now in detail under four separate heads.

1. The president conceded that the policies of the previous 39 years in respect of (a) the citizenship and voting rights of the Tamil plantation-worker population, and (b) the "Sinhala only" language policy were mistaken and injurious not only to the people affected

but to the Sinhala people as well and so, would be reversed. In announcing this decision he uttered his now famous *mea culpa*,taking on himself, personally, much of the blame for these policies.

2. He abandoned the clearly-stated and oft-repeated policies in respect of (a) Indian intervention in the domestic affairs of Sri Lanka. Having opposed Indian involvement, let alone intervention, uncompromisingly he now invited Indian troops into the island to disarm the Tamil militants. And (b) The combination of the northern and eastern provinces which together form the territory of the state of Eelam. Having rejected the demand of the Tamil people for this combination out of hand, he now agreed to it as a temporary measure until a referendum on it was held (it has proved irreversible and is in force to this day).

3. Such an abrupt about-turn by the ship of state was decided on in the utmost secrecy, without consultation with his own party, or cabinet, or Prime Minister or Parliament, let alone the public at large. And it was done while an All-Party Conference was waffling on interminably for years, unable to decide on an agreed and coherent policy on the ethnic question. It demonstrated conclusively the effectiveness of the presidential initiative as against the impotence of Parliament with its competing political parties playing to the nationalist, xenophobic gallery.

4. The entire package of changes in policies both external and domestic was intensely unpopular among all the Sinhala political parties including the President's own; in Parliament where his party had five-sixths of the seats only two ministers supported the President and all the rest were opposed to him. The public took to the streets to demonstrate their anger and the extreme Sinhala JVP revolutionary party went on a rampage of destruction of government property and launched an open attempt to overthrow the government. The man who had ridden the crest of the wave of victory triumphantly at the 1977 general election stood totally isolated with 99 per cent of the Sinhala people against him. In a now-famous BBC broadcast from London on the morning after these changes had been announced in Colombo, the President of the Sinhala Association in London denounced them as the greatest betrayal of the Sinhala race in its 2500-year history.

For any political leader to weather such a storm would be a near-miracle. But weather it he did. And the sole reason for his survival was that in the contest of wills it was Parliament that cracked and backed down. Legislative effect was given to the announced changes and the statute book was purged of the raft of discriminatory legislation that had led to war.

Even more amazing was the eventual acceptance by the public at large and all the Sinhala political parties of the total reversal in domestic policies. Today not even the most extreme chauvinistic Sinhala political party or group espouses a return to the status quo ante 1987; no one proposes to render the Tamil plantation-worker population stateless and voteless; no one asks for Sinhala Only — three official languages for the state is a universally accepted reality.

Few democracies can have experienced such traumatic upheavals in constitutional form and domestic policies. If anybody of voters can be said to be tempered to meet the challenge of radical change it is the Sinhala public.

What happened in July 1987 is unquestionably the most significant political event since independence and its many paradoxes resonate to this day. For instance, the President's action was thoroughly elitist and undemocratic and yet it was manifestly in the national interest, especially that of the Sinhala people. Also it was thoroughly unpopular among the Sinhala people and roused them into a furious opposition unprecedented in recent history and yet after the fait accompli it is now universally accepted. On the other hand its greatest benefit for the Sinhala people is insufficiently recognised and seldom openly mentioned; and that is that it delivered them from the mortal danger of the plantation Tamil population opting for an armed struggle or asking for a state of their own. For that reason alone President Jayawardene has earned the lasting gratitude of the Sinhala people.

On the external front, however, the volte-face of July 1987 failed because it aimed at preserving the status quo i.e. the British unitary state of Ceylon, and at disarming the Tamil people in order to force them against their expressed will into an artificial state which was nothing more than an imperial relict. Even if the Indian forces had succeeded in disarming the LTTE all they would have achieved would have been the further inflammation of Tamil nationalism (including that in Tamilnadu itself) rather than the suppression of it. The misreading of the root cause of the war contained the seeds of the failure of the first President's bold initiative in respect of its principal object, namely, the victorious conclusion of the war.

It is instructive at this stage to pause to consider the attitude of the Sinhala people to two crucial issues — the "Sinhala Only" language policy and the war. On both there has been impressive bi-partisan political unanimity among the Sinhala political parties. Mr. S.W.R.D. Bandaranaike is often blamed for the Sinhala Only language policy but in fact the tide of public opinion in favour of that policy ran so strong in the mid-fifties that it swept along all the Sinhala political parties with it. In the 1956 general election both the SLFP and the UNP espoused the Sinhala Only policy. The disastrous consequences of that policy, the fact that it has led to war and the subconscious intuition that it was fundamentally unethical, have all combined to bring about its universal abandonment.

The war, on the other hand, has not the immediate impact on the daily lives of the Sinhala people as did the Sinhala Only policy. For most Sinhala people the war is a distant disturbance, taking place far away, its sights and sounds carefully screened out from their cognition by the government-owned media. There is no fighting in the seven Sinhala-occupied provinces. There is no perceived threat to hearth and home or livelihood. The situation of the Sinhala people in the north-east province is not a burning issue. It is not a people's war in which they have risen to take arms; it is a war conducted by their government with a professional army.

From the policy of Sinhala Only the Sinhala people expected great benefits, not least economic and material in the form of government jobs and employment in the private sector. They would be hard put to it to discern what benefits can be expected from the war which is conducted largely with imported weaponry costing the earth in hard-won foreign exchange. And yet the policy of Sinhala Only was abandoned without a qualm when its futility was perceived. There is little reason to believe that the transition from war to peace will be less welcome.

At his inauguration in January 1989 President Premadasa vowed to uphold the territorial integrity of the country. Presidential pronouncements of this kind have an interesting history, not least in recent times. President Mitterrand was elected promising sweeping socialism and then presided over a government moving distinctly rightwards and delivering to the French people unprecedented progress and prosperity. President Bush asked his listeners to "Read my lips" when he offered no new taxes but he had to eat those words. President Gorbachev resolved to preserve the Soviet Union and had to preside perforce over its dismantling. Mr Major announced that he would take Britain to the heart of Europe and is busy entrenching Britain at its periphery. Presidential pronounce-ments of this kind invariably focus on the area of greatest uncer-tainty in the minds both of the president making the pronounce-ment and of the public at which it is directed, and they are intended to reassure both. And, as in the instances mentioned above, the tide of events has led to reversal when the national interest has so demanded. Pragmatism has prevailed over presidential pronounce-ments and that is what good government is all about.

In the final analysis it is the national interest of the Sinhala nation that will prevail and it is an interest to which President Premadasa was keenly attuned. He had given a clearer indication of pragma-tism in the national interest than any of his predecessors and one which revealed that his reading of the national interest gives primacy to the relief of the poor and their elevation to prosperity. He removed the 100 per cent tax on foreign private investment in Sri Lankan enterprises which had acted as a nearly insuperable disin-centive to such investment despite all the blandishments to attract it. This showed that he realised the enormous potential of foreign private investment as opposed to the limited and conditional hand-outs of multilateral institutions such as the IMF, the World Bank, the Asian Development Bank, the Paris Consortium etc. It showed also that he is willing to pay the price for such investment which is foreign ownership of productive assets in Sri Lanka in order to secure its benefits for the poor. All previous governments while inviting foreign private investment in theory, discouraged it in practice in order to retain ownership in national (i.e. national middle class or upper class) hands thus condemning those who could benefit from such investment to continuance in abject pov-erty. President Premadasa started from the other end. He worked towards ending abject poverty and was ready to pay the price for it. Essentially a pragmatist not a purblind nationalist, in a contest between nationalism and poverty alleviation, it is for the latter that he opted every time.

The war now raging is the greatest impediment to the alleviation of poverty and to rapid economic growth which could, in time, eliminate rather than alleviate poverty. Peace will utterly transform the prospects for economic growth and enable rapid industrialisation — the vast Indian market now opening up next door is a new opportunity urgently to be sieged — modernisation of the infrastructure, education etc,. Premadasa had the historic opportunity for ending it by taking an initiative similar to, but even more significant than, that taken by Jayawardene. Whereas that initiative was flawed from the outset by its attempt to preserve a status quo which had already vanished except for those in the grip of the dead hand of the past, an initiative by President Premadasa to recognise the stark reality of the existence now of two states on the island each with an army of its own, would have been a forward-looking act of statesmanship which would have laid the foundation for two prosperous and progressive nation-states living side-by-side in good neighbourliness and concord as do most of the nations of the world. Whereas Jayawardene's initiative failed, President Premadasa's initiative could have gone down in history as the true salvation of the Sinhala people and he could claim justifiably to be the real father of the state which will then have every right to the name of Sri Lanka.

In our consideration of Jayawardene's initiative we saw that his five-sixths majority in Parliament enabled him to get legislative sanction for his initiative even though Parliament was, at first, unanimously hostile. President Premadasa had no such easy passage through Parliament. He had to go over Parliament's head directly to the people in a referendum to secure their approval for the fait accompli of his recognition of the state of Eelam and the terms of peace with that state. These would have had to be concluded with the same swiftness and finality as was Jayawardene's Peace Accord with the Indian government.

President Premadasa had the goodwill and trust of the great majority of the ordinary people of the country. He had the eloquence to explain to them where their true interests lie and what the ushering in of peace will do for them. He had the services of the media for conveying to the public at large the need for such a new departure. His demarche would have been altogether more democratic than Jayawardene's was in 1987. It would not have incurred the opprobrium of bringing in foreign troops into the country and depending on them to secure a national goal. Coming to terms with a stark reality will be less damaging to the Sinhala psyche than seeing the Sinhala language dethroned from its pre-eminence. The latter, far more severe blow brought no material compensation to the Sinhala people whereas peace with separation will bring them benefits undreamt of up to now and, best of all, deliverance from a conflict in which the moral balance is tipped against them.

When carried in a referendum, parliamentary approval for the will of the people will be a formality and a new era in the history of the Sinhala nation will commence. The President's standing in the international community would have soared to world leadership levels that no ruler of Sri Lanka has ever achieved in history and both Sri Lanka and Eelam would have been welcomed into the family of nations as shining examples of the peaceful and far-sighted resolution of nationalist aspirations.

After the long nightmare of war, by a single final act of a Sinhala leader, the future happiness, tranquillity and prosperity of the Sinhala people would have been assured.

Epilogue

It is inevitable that a book such as this should be overtaken by events that take place between writing and publication. They affect both the personalities in the living drama and the book's main thesis.

Where the personalities are concerned the changes were tragic and sensational. President Premadasa was assassinated on 1st May 1993 and was succeeded that same day by Mr D.B. Wijetunga who was Prime Minister at the time. The LTTE is regarded as the organisation responsible for funding and supplying the presumed perpetrator of the deed, a young Tamil man who had wormed his way into Mr Premadasa's confidence. In his last year in office Mr Premadasa had alienated many elements of the Sinhala elite especially within his own party. He was increasingly dependent on the Tamil political party within the government — the Ceylon Workers Congress and its leader Mr Thondaman who commanded the plantation Tamil vote. Also the anti-LTTE Tamil political parties which had left the north-east (or had been expelled therefrom by the LTTE as traitors to the cause of a separate, sovereign, Tamil state, Eelam) and had moved to Colombo and become clients of the government were regarded by Mr Premadasa as more reliable allies than Sinhala politicians. At such a conjuncture why the LTTE should have inspired the assassination is still a mystery. It is rumoured that there were secret dealings between Mr Premadasa and the LTTE possibly through the suspected assassin himself. Since the assassination removed in one blow all those who could have been privy to such dealings on the Sinhala side the mystery is likely to remain just that until a definitive LTTE version of such dealings, if any, surfaces many years hence.

The new President, Mr Wijetunga, is a much more acceptable figure in the conservative Sinhala political milieu than Mr Premadasa. He is a member of the upper caste (Govigama) of the Sinhala people; he is a conventional Buddhist with none of Mr Premadasa's predeliction towards Hindu syncretism. He has an easier and more comfortable rapport with Sinhala nationalism coming as he does from a deeply rural background unlike Mr Premadasa who had emerged from Colombo's concrete jungle. These, however, are differences more of nuance than of substance. In the last resort they are very similar experienced politicians with a pragmatic cast of mind.

So much for the personalities involved.

Events between the end of 1991 and the present time have re-inforced this book's main thesis — that it is only by a bold presidential initiative that peace can be obtained.

A Parliamentary Select Committee headed by Mr Mangala Moonesinghe, M.P. of the SLFP (the leading party in the opposition) has concluded its work and submitted a report which aims to go back to colonial times in respect of the provincial structure i.e. to revert to a separate northern province and a separate eastern province as set up by the British. It does propose a devolution of powers on the lines of the Indian Constitution while carefully avoiding the word "federal". It claims that both main Sinhala political parties — UNP and SLFP — are agreeable to this even though both had refused to submit specific proposals to the Select Committee. After the report was submitted both parties have been very guarded in their pronouncements regarding the recommenda-tions. All the Tamil political parties which participated in the Committee's proceedings have rejected the proposal to de-merge the two provinces. The LTTE, though invited by the Committee to present its proposals, ignored the request. The Select Committee did not address the crucial question of how a federal or quasi-federal proposal could deal with or answer a situation which was now manifestly post-federal in that the party sought to be included in the federation was armed and could not be disarmed even by the use of force.

The Select Committee proved beyond any possible doubt that no worthwhile or credible initiative for securing peace could emanate from Parliament. Parliament as an institution, and every political party in it, is unable to contemplate the securing of peace through separation into two independent, sovereign states. In this they faithfully represent the overwhelming mass of the Sinhala people in whose political discourse even the mere mention of peace through separation is taboo. There is not the slightest hint of awareness that in other parts of the world in every case where nationalist guerilla wars for the establishment of a separate state have ended they have ended by the establishment of the separate state fought for by the guerillas. The background to the establishment of the Irish Republic in 1922 after a near-identical conflict to that in Sri Lanka is never mentioned. The break-up of the Ethiopian state and the establishment of the state of Eritrea in 1993 is never mentioned. The numerous instances of empires and states disintegrating under nationalist pressure (either overtly exerted militarily or just threatened) are ignored.

It is this kind of failure of liberal democratic parliamentary systems that has led to the emergence of an executive presidency vested with the power and the right to take a gridlock-breaking initiative in the long term national interest. The classic example is the Fourth Republic in France, bogged down in the seemingly interminable and certainly unwinnable Algerian war of independence. The impasse was broken only by the emergence of the Fifth Republic under Charles de Gaulle. He exercised the presidential initiative decisively in ending the Algerian war by recognising the independence of Algeria; he made the historic move to reinstate defeated and disgraced Germany in the European comity of nations — both were extremely unpopular measures at the time — and to set France on its course to its present eminence and prosperity. The raison d'etre of the presidential system of government is its role in compensating for the infirmity of Parliament by courageous, statesman like, prescient departures which though thoroughly unpopular at the time are manifestly required to return a nation to its true destiny. Of course it needs a man who is big enough to answer the call to greatness. That is its weakness and its strength.

In the meantime, on the field of battle, the world's universal experience of the inadequacy of conventional armies ranged against highly-motivated nationalist guerillas on the latter's homeground, is being re-enacted. The Sri Lanka army has suffered a series of military reverses which have dissipated the delusion that the war could be quickly and overwhelmingly won. The unthinkable thought whether it could be won at all lurks hauntingly in the background. The military leaders' oft-repeated assurances of imminent military victory have turned to dust and ashes in their mouths.

The public mind (including that of politicians of all stripes) seems to find it difficult to comprehend the fundamental, systemic difference between a nationalist guerilla war on the one hand and an ideological guerilla insurgency on the other. The former aims at establishing a separate, sovereign, independent state in a territory occupied mainly by its nation. The latter has no such objective. Instead it aims to change the power structure both in the state and in the society in which it is located. For the Sinhala people the difficulty of comprehending this distinction is compounded by their recent experience of the latter i.e. an ideological movement — the JVP. The fact that the JVP was crushed militarily leads them to the facile conclusion that the nationalist guerilla movement of the LTTE could, perhaps even in the long run, be extirpated by military force. The fact that an armed guerilla movement fighting for a separate state has never been extinguished by the superior force of a conventional army or even forced to relinquish its primary goal and settle for a lesser deal is not part of the public consciousness.

So the conflict drags on — at a cost of around Rs. 70 million a day (the 1993 figure) to the exchequer. All of the government's social amelioration programmes are affected in one way or another — phased out (the janasaviya), postponed or scaled down. The election promise of electrifying a small part of the railway network (Sri Lanka has not a mile of electrified line at present) has remained on paper. Contrariwise, when the Air Force asks for funds for the purchase of six Hercules transport aircraft it is refused and told "the life of the community must go on". The war is not everything; there are even more important objectives to ensure that the governing party stays in power. In the trade-off between pragmatism and militaristic nationalism the former still has a small edge.

The Sinhala political elite is well aware how far their country lags behind the emerging economic power-houses of Asia — the ASEAN Six, South Korea, the Overseas Chinese bastions of Hongkong and Taiwan and, even resurgent Vietnam. The only one of them that is not at peace is the Philippines and it is the "sick man" among them. The causal relationship between peace and prosperity is now well-known; conversely, persistence in an unwinnable war condemns the Sinhala people to glaring inferiority to their fast-developing neighbours by every measure of the quality of life and well-being.

The government is sensitive, also, to the international reaction to the continuance, and possible escalation, of warfare. This is one of the very real constraints under which the war is being waged. The damage caused to civil establishments by aerial bombing arouses international attention. A resurgence of refugees into Tamilnadu will revive the old demands for Indian intervention to enforce a pax indica on both sides if not to establish the state of Eelam.

The Sinhala leadership is notably pragmatic when it eventually awakes to the realities of a situation. It has shown itself to be astute enough to make a virtue of necessity. The best, indeed the only, hope for peace on the island lies in the recognition by the President of the final denouement towards which the inexorable tide of events is moving — separation into two states and a prescient initiative by him to manage that conclusion in the true national interests of the Sinhala people. He can present to them a clear rationale for such an initiative; one that had proved successful everywhere else and will bear the same fruits in Sri Lanka as well. Only thus can the long nightmare be brought to an end and the Sinhala nation set on the path to the sunlit uplands of peace and prosperity.

Index